C000156723

A Pol

Recollections ᴏ. ᴊamuel Waters, RIC

IRISH NARRATIVES

IRISH NARRATIVES

Series edited by David Fitzpatrick

Personal narratives of past lives are essential for understanding any field of history. They provide unrivalled insight into the day-to-day consequences of political, social, economic or cultural relationships. Memoirs, diaries and personal letters, whether by public figures or obscure witnesses of historical events, will often captivate the general reader as well as engrossing the specialist. Yet the vast majority of such narratives are preserved only among the manuscripts or rarities in libraries and archives scattered over the globe. The aim of this series of brief yet scholarly editions is to make available a wide range of narratives concerning Ireland and the Irish over the last four centuries. All documents, or sets of documents, are edited and introduced by specialist scholars, who guide the reader through the world in which the text was created. The chosen texts are faithfully transcribed, the biographical and local background explored, and the documents set in historical context. This series will prove invaluable for university and school teachers, providing superb material for essays and textual analysis in class. Above all, it offers a novel opportunity for readers interested in Irish history to discover fresh and exciting sources of personal testimony.

Other titles in the series:

Andrew Bryson's Ordeal: An Epilogue to the 1798 Rebellion, edited by Michael Durey
Henry Stratford Persse's Letters from Galway to America, 1821–1832, edited by James L. Pethica and James C. Roy
A Redemptorist Missionary in Ireland, 1851–1854: Memoirs by Joseph Prost, translated and edited by Emmet Larkin and Herman Freudenberger
Frank Henderson's Easter Rising, edited by Michael Hopkinson
A Patriot Priest: The Life of Father James Coigly, 1761–1798, edited by Dáire Keogh
The Rebel in his Family: Selected Papers of William Smith O'Brien, edited by Richard and Marianne Davis
'My Darling Danny': Letters from Mary O'Connell to her son Daniel, 1830–1832, edited by Erin I. Bishop
The Reynolds Letters: An Irish Emigrant Family in Late Victorian Manchester, edited by Lawrence W. McBride
'The Misfit Soldier': Edward Casey's War Story, 1914–1918, edited by Joanna Bourke

Forthcoming titles:

Alfred Webb: The Autobiography of a Quaker Nationalist, edited by Marie-Louise Legg

David Fitzpatrick teaches history at Trinity College, Dublin. His books include *Politics and Irish Life, 1913–1921* (1977, reissued 1998) and *Oceans of Consolation: Personal Accounts of Irish Migration to Australia* (1995).

A Policeman's Ireland
Recollections of Samuel Waters, RIC

Edited by
Stephen Ball

CORK UNIVERSITY PRESS

First published in 1999 by
Cork University Press
Cork
Ireland

British Library Cataloguing in Publication Data

ISBN 1 85918 189 9

Typesetting by Red Barn Publishing, Skeagh, Skibbereen

Reprinted in 2005 by Lightning Source, UK

Contents

Acknowledgements

The original typescript of the memoirs of Samuel Waters is in the Public Record Office of Northern Ireland (Gore-Booth Papers, D/4051/14). It is a copy of this document that I used in preparing the manuscript for publication. I gratefully acknowledge the permission of the Deputy Keeper of the Records to publish this document. Ultimate copyright remains in the hands of the Gore-Booth family, and I wish to thank Sir Josslyn Gore-Booth for his permission to publish the memoir.

I am grateful to the staff of the National Archives and the National Library of Ireland for their assistance in providing me with supplementary documentation from their collections. I would also like to thank the general editor of the *Irish Narratives* series, Professor David Fitzpatrick, for his comments, guidance and advice throughout the writing of this project.

My interest in Samuel Waters arose during research for my Ph.D thesis 'Policing the Land War: British Government Policy towards Political Protest and Agrarian Crime in Ireland, 1879–92', which was supervised by Professor David Killingray at Goldsmith's College, University of London, between 1994 and 1998. I wish to thank him for his wise counsel during this period, and also to express my gratitude to the British Academy and the Institute of Historical Research for their financial assistance.

Finally, I would like to thank Donald Ball for his patient assistance in preparing the maps for this publication.

Introduction

> The history of my life — I wonder! Will it ever be written, and, if ever written, will it be worth reading?

So begins this short memoir written in 1924 by Samuel Abraham Walker Waters. His memoir is a rare example of an autobiography by a Royal Irish Constabulary officer, and it provides a valuable insight into the organisation that policed Ireland for one hundred years between 1822 and 1922. Samuel Waters rose steadily through the officer ranks to become an Assistant Inspector-General. He lived through a period of great social and political change: he was born in 1846 during the Great Famine and died in 1936 as a citizen of the Irish Free State. Waters not only recollects his own life but also reviews the times through which he lived. Waters joined the Constabulary in 1866, shortly before the Fenian rising, and continued to serve the government, undertaking intermittent intelligence assignments, until 1920, the eve of Irish independence. His memoir contains a personal account of important historic events such as the Fenian rising, the Land War, the Special Commission on Parnellism and crime, the Easter Rising and the Anglo-Irish War. Waters drew upon his personal participation in these events, and he provides a valuable and unique perspective on Irish life between 1850 and 1920.

The document is a memoir in its essential sense as a simple, unadorned autobiographical record of actions, events and experiences. It combines personal reminiscences of Waters's childhood, education, personal development and private life with a retrospective account of his professional career during which he became personally acquainted with the hidden springs of governmental power. He wrote the memoir for his family: it was not intended for publication and is therefore artless and frequently candid. Although he looks back over a period of sixty years, he gives a remarkably accurate account of his career, apart from a handful of minor discrepancies. As a police officer, Waters was well practised in the art of recording events, and many of his

recollections are supported by supplementary documentation preserved in official records. He wrote the memoir in a clear and eco-
nomical style that provides a brisk and engaging narrative and reveals
the author's genial personality. As a policeman, Waters travelled widely
about Ireland and came into contact with all classes of Irish society. His
recollections illuminate many diverse aspects of Irish life in the late
nineteenth and early twentieth centuries. His account sets the Royal
Irish Constabulary into a social and political context.

Waters was frequently transferred and for many years led a peripatetic life. He was posted to eleven stations in nine different counties
and served in all four provinces of Ireland. The memoir contains
diverse social observations, which range from the sporting and social
activities of the Anglo-Irish gentry to village life in rural Ireland, and
records the conventions, manners and class relationships of nineteenth-
century Ireland. Waters's police duties were many and varied. He took
part in 'quelling riots', 'arresting Fenians' and 'poteen hunting' in
Sligo. He also witnessed sectarian conflict in Tyrone and agrarian disturbances in Westmeath during the Land War before embarking upon
a career in the Constabulary's 'Special Branch', where he pioneered the
development of police intelligence-gathering. During his long career
Waters met many colourful characters, including the Irish-American
Fenian, Colonel Ricard Burke, and developed friendships with nationalist politicians. He was also personally acquainted with leading con-
temporary British politicans and administrators such as Sir Antony
MacDonnell, George Wyndham and Arthur Balfour.

Waters offers an uncommon perspective on the struggle for
national independence in Ireland. He was an Irish policeman committed to the preservation of the Union between Great Britain and Ireland, and accordingly devoted himself to the suppression of Irish
republicanism. Like many Irish policemen, Samuel Waters came from
a 'police family'. Three generations of the Waters family served in the
Constabulary, and their careers span the entire history of the force. In
1786 the government established a force of 750 police officers in
Dublin. This controversial innovation created the first full-time police

force in the British Isles. In 1808 the government transferred control of this force to the city magistrates, who appointed 200 patrolling constables known as 'peace officers'. One of these constables was Samuel's grandfather, William Waters. William was born in County Wicklow in 1789 and became a peace officer for the Castle Division of Dublin in March 1810. In 1814 the Irish Chief Secretary, Robert Peel, established the Peace Preservation Force, a semi-military police force which the government employed to suppress agrarian and sectarian disorder in 'proclaimed' districts.[1] In February 1820 William Waters joined this force as a Chief Constable. He remained in it until 1836, when the government merged the Peace Preservation Force with the County Constabulary, which had been established in 1822. This reform created the Irish Constabulary, a unitary, centrally controlled police force of 10,000 armed men that policed Ireland until its disbandment in 1922.[2] William Waters joined the Irish Constabulary as Chief Constable for the Ballynahinch district of County Down, where he had served with the Peace Preservation Force since 1828.[3] However, William did not last long in the new Constabulary. Although the local magistrates considered him to be an urbane, impartial and efficient officer, the government believed that, at the age of fifty, William was past his best. His physical infirmities caused him to neglect his duties, and in October 1840 he was dismissed from the force. Although the government granted William a pension, he had no private means to supplement it and had to struggle to support his family. He pleaded to be reinstated, and beseeched the Under-Secretary, Norman Macdonald, thus: 'I crave mercy and pardon which has been often granted to persons under sentence of Death, and my sentence is the same to me as Death — and I trust that you will say it is too severe for my crime.' However, the Chief Secretary, Viscount Morpeth, would not allow William back into the Constabulary, offering instead to fund his passage to the colonies, an offer which William declined.[4]

Five years earlier William's son, Abraham, had joined his father in the Constabulary as a Sub-Constable, having, as Samuel tells it, refused an offer to take William's place as an Inspector. Abraham quickly rose through the ranks and was promoted to Sub-Inspector on 13 October 1846.[5] Samuel was born just one week later in Ferbane, King's County (Offaly), and shortly afterwards the family moved to Carrick-on-Shannon, where Samuel spent his early childhood before going to school in Edinburgh and then to work as a shipping clerk in London. However, when Samuel reached the age of eighteen, he decided to return to Ireland in order to compete for a cadetship in the Constabulary.

The Irish Constabulary was a native police force under the British Crown — in the words of one policeman's son, 'a force of Irishmen with the duty of maintaining peace and order in their homeland'.[6] Its rank and file came mainly from the Irish countryside; most recruits were the sons of tenant farmers or rural labourers who joined the force for regular employment and the promise of a pension. However, the government perceived that the predominantly Catholic rank and file might be torn between attachment to their class or nation and their allegiance to the Crown. The Irish Constabulary was an armed force that was trained, organised and disciplined on military lines, and its men were widely distributed in 1,500 barracks across Ireland where they often faced peculiarly irksome duties. The government therefore considered it necessary to create an officer cadre whose social status and education would provide them with sufficient authority to control a large body of armed men dispersed in small stations. The officer class was composed of about 200 Sub-Inspectors and 35 County Inspectors. They were largely Protestant Irishmen who owed their allegiance firmly to the British government.[7] Most of them were commissioned to their rank from outside the force and trained as cadets. The rigid class barrier between officers and men did little to foster a community of feeling between them. The cadet system was introduced in 1842, and general opposition to it from the ranks gradually increased. By the turn of the century the inspectorate was widely regarded as outmoded, and frequent calls were made for it to be abolished. Officers were ridiculed in the press as 'the golf-monocle section of the Force' and were denounced for their bigotry, arrogance and intolerance. In

1914 a constable complained: 'These officers are taken from the ruling classes and they look upon the rank and file with the greatest contempt.'[8] The cadet system was retained, but the number of promotions from the ranks was steadily increased.[9]

Cadets were selected according to a rigorous competitive examination that often required six months of preparation, working twelve-hour days with a Dublin 'grinder'.[10] The candidates were generally well-educated young men in their early twenties. A significant number of them were university graduates, former government clerks and ex-military officers. Most had links with landed gentry in their family backgrounds. They were the sons of Protestant clergymen, magistrates and professionals, families at 'the lower end of the higher social scale' who could not afford army commissions.[11] Successful candidates spent four to five months at the Constabulary Depot in Phoenix Park. They were instructed in drill, writing reports and keeping accounts, a form of training more suitable for infantry officers than policemen.[12] Nevertheless, the government expected to gain advantage from having at its disposal 'a body of Junior Officers drawn from a high spirited class — well educated and highly trained in professional and general acquirements — and capable of as gallant and difficult achievements as any body of officers in the world'.[13]

A Sub-Inspector's duties were responsible but not exacting. Under ordinary circumstances, there was little serious crime in rural areas. In the 1860s an officer's most demanding task was to keep order at elections, and Waters witnessed a particularly violent one in Sligo in 1868 (pp. 31, 36).[14] Voting was conducted openly and continued for more than a week. One Constabulary officer recalled that 'There was a belief, almost amounting to an understanding that there was "No Law" during an Election, the rival candidates were supported by bands of fighting men armed with guns, pistols and bludgeons.'[15] After the Ballot Act was introduced in 1872 elections were usually much less violent affairs. Apart from occasionally supervising his men in keeping the peace at fairs or evictions, an officer's duties might be confined to conducting monthly barrack inspections.

Samuel Waters appears to have had plenty of spare time with which to pursue a range of sporting activities. Field sports were a vitally important part of many Constabulary officers' lives, particularly in remote rural postings where there was usually little else to do. Waters developed a love of outdoor sports at an early age and became passionately devoted to hunting, shooting, fishing, sailing and swimming. He devoted every spare hour to these pursuits, and consequently he recalls some of the encounters he had with gamekeepers and bailiffs. Waters was also a missionary for cricket in Ireland. He cleared a patch of ground for a pitch wherever he could, before inducting his men into the mysteries of the game and taking on the soldiers of the local garrison in challenge matches. Unfortunately his teams were rarely a match for the troops. Waters recounts that a group of local Fenians once offered to employ 'physical force' on his behalf so as to prevent an inevitable defeat (pp. 28–29). Sport appears to have played an important role in cementing relations between the police and the community. When Waters was the County Inspector in Kerry, he co-operated with the Gaelic Athletic Association to put on an annual police sports day at Tralee (p. 76). When a similar event was held in Cork in June 1890, a confidential report recorded that men of all shades of political opinion identified themselves with these sports. These occasions also provided the local gentry with an opportunity to display their solidarity with the forces of law and order. The Divisional Commissioner recorded that the event was 'well patronized, especially by the better classes, who do not normally attend such gatherings, but put in an appearance in large numbers on this occasion out of compliment to the Constabulary'.[16] Later in life Waters developed an interest in golf and croquet, eventually becoming a champion player and honorary secretary of the Irish Croquet Association. His love for sport brought him into the social circle of well-known Anglo-Irish families. Social intercourse with the local gentry was vital if a Constabulary officer was to retain the confidence of the landed class and the magistracy. While he was stationed at Grange, County Sligo, in the late 1860s, Waters was a frequent guest at Lissadell, the country house of the Gore-Booth family, 'that old

Georgian mansion' later eulogised by William Butler Yeats.[17] He took part in grouse-shooting, fox-hunting and, less conventionally, in rat-catching, as a member of the 'Pig and Whistle Club' which policed Lissadell's verminous kitchens (p. 32).

Nevertheless, life could also be a struggle for a young police officer. Waters eventually reared a large family of ten daughters and three sons,[18] and he admitted to being 'hard up' for much of his career. Junior officers without private incomes struggled to aspire to the rank of 'gentleman'. A Sub-Inspector's annual salary of £125 barely supported Waters's lively social life, which involved attending balls and gambling with military officers. His problems with money began during training at the Depot when he had to resort to moneylenders in order to settle his mess bills, and indebtedness soon got him into trouble with his superiors. While Waters claims that his Head Constable's ignorance of regulations caused his transfer from his much-loved first posting in Grange (p. 30), the official records tell a different story. It is true that the district did receive unfavourable reports following the general inspections of 1869 and 1870, but it was Waters's impecuniosity that caused his transfer. When local magistrates tried to keep Waters in Grange, the Inspector-General, Sir John Stewart Wood, informed them: 'I moved Sub Inspector Waters from Grange in consequence of his having borrowed a sum of money from a Gentleman in the neighbourhood — and feeling satisfied that no officer can do his duty properly and independently who is under pecuniary obligation to anyone in his District.'[19] Waters's financial difficulties persisted, and three years later he received another unfavourable record for misappropriating public money and not paying his men on time.[20] His unorthodox accounting practices grew out of genuine hardship, living as he did on a fixed income at a time of rising prices. As a young father stationed in south Cork in 1874, he was forced to make his own furniture and live off the fish and fowl he managed to catch. Shortage of money also forced him to adopt some less attractive methods of raising cash. Waters cheerfully admits to having connived with a local doctor and a magistrate to report trivial drunken brawls as serious assaults. As a result, the cases were tried at the Cork assizes, which allowed him to claim travelling and accommodation expenses and have 'a high old time in the city' (p. 43).

Waters provides valuable insights into the daily routines of the police service. He demonstrates that, during times of social peace, the Constabulary functioned as a normal civil police force. It undertook routine duties to prevent drunkenness and petty theft, inspect weights and measures, collect statistics and enforce licensing laws. This qualifies the common perception of the RIC as a predominantly paramilitary force engaged in the suppression of political unrest.[21] Waters also demonstrates that junior officers were not particularly well trained in police duties and relied heavily upon their Head Constables to conduct the day-to-day administration of their districts. Waters described his own Head Constable as a man whose 'hazy perception of the technical regulations of the Force' did not prevent him from keeping order in his sub-district (p. 29). This perhaps illustrates that the policing of rural Ireland could be flexible and pragmatic. The novelist 'George A. Birmingham' (Canon J. O. Hannay) concluded his comparison of the English and Irish styles of policing thus: 'The Irish policeman is a more philosophic man. He considers, before he attempts to enforce a law, where the balance of convenience lies.'[22] The RIC was a strictly disciplined police force with military capabilities. However, it is also evident that Irish policemen were not necessarily hidebound by regulations. They were often prepared to bend the rules to suit the needs and disposition of the rural community.

Nevertheless, in a country where there was great potential for social and political conflict, policing also had to have a sterner aspect. Whenever conflict arose and the law lost popular legitimacy, the role of the police became controversial. Birmingham argued that the English people regarded the law as their own creation, devised for their own convenience, and only employed to punish criminals; whereas in Ireland 'every one is a potential malefactor. We are not supposed to love the law which was made for us and not by us. It is desirable only that we should fear it.'[23] The men of the RIC were capable of maintaining that fear. The Irish police were the basis of official power in Ireland and formed the very root of the legal machine. The RIC was well trained, highly disciplined, efficient and guided by professional standards of behaviour. Even during times of social strife it served the government faithfully. Following the Land War, one former Head Constable remarked: 'To the government we have been more than subjects, we were the best Police force in Europe — subordinate, loyal, and uncompromising.'[24] Wherever popular support for the law was uncertain, the government discouraged any familiarity with its embodiment, the policeman. The Constabulary's ranks were filled with members of the 'peasantry', and the authorities wished to segregate them from their own communities. The men were not allowed to serve in their native counties and were housed in remote barracks. These arrangements were designed to ensure loyalty and impartiality; but they also reinforced prejudices. During times of communal strife the RIC was popularly represented as the instrument of the landlords and the government in Dublin Castle. In 1890, when the Irish Home Rule MP Alfred Webb spoke out against the 'irresponsible Bashi-Bazouk action of the police in Ireland', he described the RIC as 'an incubus upon all civil life with no effective control over it. It is a Force which, though nominally Irish, is not Irish in feeling or tradition or any of its connections. It is among us, but not of us.'[25] While such sentiments were never universal, they do represent an attitude that was to become widespread before the Constabulary's demise in 1922.

Waters's first experience of political unrest came very early in his career. In 1867 he helped to frustrate the '*Jackmel* expedition', an abortive invasion of Ireland by Irish-American Fenians and one of the rising's most celebrated episodes. On 15 March 1867 the Fenian leader Colonel Thomas J. Kelly appealed to the military council in New York to mount an expedition to land men and arms on the coast of Sligo. It was intended to provide support for their Irish colleagues who had launched the rebellion on 5 March. They quickly obtained a 138-ton brigantine called the *Jackmel Packet*, which set sail for Ireland on 13 April, loaded with arms and a military force of thirty-eight men led by Colonel William Nagle. Kelly dispatched his secretary, Captain Ricard

Burke, from England to meet the *Jackmel* on its arrival. Burke spent several weeks in Sligo posing as a Scottish touring artist named 'Mr Walters'. He frequented the billiard rooms of the town, and even played an occasional game with the local Resident Magistrate. Burke hired a small hooker in Mullaghmore, ostensibly for sailing and fishing excursions, and traversed Sligo Bay watching out for the *Jackmel*. At this point Waters interviewed Burke but, seeing Burke's letter of introduction from the Resident Magistrate, decided not to interfere with him. The *Jackmel*, now rechristened *Erin's Hope*, entered Sligo Bay on 23 May 1867. Two days later Burke met the vessel and told Nagle that the rising in Sligo had already been suppressed and advised him to sail south. Two members of the *Jackmel*'s crew who had been injured in a shooting accident were put ashore, where they were promptly arrested by Waters, who then alerted the authorities. By the time the brig reached the coast of County Waterford it was short of provisions, and the crew voted to return to the United States. On 1 June thirty-two of the men went ashore at Helvick Head, near Dungarvan Bay, but they were quickly arrested.[26] The failure to apprehend Burke in Sligo had fateful consequences. He returned to England and on 18 September staged the rescue of Colonel Thomas J. Kelly and Captain Timothy Deasy from the custody of the Manchester police. During the rescue a policeman, Sergeant Charles Brett, was shot dead. William Allen, Michael Larkin and Michael O'Brien were subsequently tried and controversially convicted of Brett's murder. They were publicly hanged on 23 November 1867 and subsequently became known as the 'Manchester Martyrs'. On the following day Burke was betrayed by the informer John Corydon and arrested in London. On 13 December 1867 his colleagues attempted to rescue him from Clerkenwell jail by breaching the prison wall with gunpowder. The explosion killed twelve people and injured more than fifty others.[27]

The years that followed the Fenian rising were relatively peaceful and prosperous in most parts of Ireland. If the country had remained tranquil, Waters might have remained a lowly Sub-Inspector. However, the great social and political upheaval of the Land War led to important changes in the organisation of the Irish police which provided the thirty-five-year-old Sub-Inspector with an opportunity for rapid advancement. His subsequent career is of particular historical interest because of his prominent role in the development of RIC Special Branch. Up to this time the Constabulary's primary task had been to preserve public order; the prevention and detection of crime were secondary considerations. The development of detective abilities was hampered by a rigid, over-centralised system of police administration that demanded 'machine-link obedience'[28] from the men and prevented them from developing the initiative necessary for successful detective work. The outburst of agrarian and political crime during the Land War of 1879–82 forced the government to develop the Constabulary's crime detection and intelli-gence-gathering capacities. Michael Davitt launched the campaign for land reform in 1879, and it transformed the political landscape of Ire-land. The Land League mobilised widespread support among the rural population and allied itself to a movement for national self-determination. As the Land League spread through the countryside, whole communities actively campaigned against landlordism and British rule. The potential for social conflict was enormous, and widespread crime and disorder accompanied the campaign.

On 1 November 1879, just ten days after the foundation of the Irish National Land League, Waters was posted to Castlepollard in County Westmeath. As tenant resistance to landlords in the district intensified, the payment of rent virtually ceased. Because the area was a stronghold of Ribbonism, the authorities believed that the Land League was using intimidation to secure its objectives. Yet the suppression of the organi-sation on 20 October 1881 merely provoked a violent reaction in many parts of Ireland. During the last two months of 1881 Westmeath wit-nessed extensive disturbances; the Castlepollard district was reported to be the 'worst and most dangerous part' of the county. Two men were shot, and eleven other agrarian outrages were committed within a short distance of the town. The authorities responded with 'sharp and ener-getic action'. Sixty troops were drafted into Castlepollard to restore order with a regular system of day and night patrols. During this emergency Waters proved himself to be a zealous officer. He arrested ten leaders of the agitation under the Protection of Person and Property Act,[29] and in February 1882 he informed the Inspector-General that he had 'established a wholesome terror amongst the dangerous class' in Castlepollard. However, repression merely forced the problem underground. At the beginning of 1882 the Special Resident Magistrate reported that 'the Ribbon Society which has always been the curse of Westmeath is again becoming active'.[30] This was to have serious consequences. On 2 April 1882 a sensational agrarian murder was committed in Waters's district at Barbavilla, near Collinstown. William Barlow Smythe had evicted a tenant named Richard Riggs, and the local Ribbon society decided to set an example to other landlords. Consequently, as Smythe and his sister-in-law were driving home from church a hidden assassin fired a shot which killed Mrs Smythe. The Barbavilla case was particularly important because it was directly linked to the 'Invincible' conspiracy to assassinate public officials in Dublin. The case largely rested upon the testimony of a father and son named McKeon and another man, Patrick Cole, all of whom claimed to have been invited to join the conspiracy. They claimed that the assassination committee had been formed on 24 March 1882 by three members of the Dublin Invincibles, Daniel Curley, Thomas Caffrey and Michael Fagan. Waters led a two-year investigation into the case. It resulted in ten local farmers being convicted for conspiracy to murder. However, William Boyhan, the man who was believed to have fired the shot, escaped to America.[31]

The Barbavilla case brought Waters to the attention of Edward Jenkinson, the man responsible for reorganising the Irish police administration. During the Land War the distinction between constitutional and revolutionary political activity was frequently unclear. Nationalist agrarian movements such as Land League and its successor, the Irish National League, were widely supported by republican secret societies which were dedicated to the violent overthrow of landlordism and British government in Ireland. Consequently, the authorities sought to improve the system of crime detection and intelligence to penetrate these underground organisations and prosecute their members. As the Land War reached a crisis in the winter of 1881–82, the government radically reorganised the police administration. The country outside Ulster was divided into six civil divisions. Each one was placed under the command of a Special Resident Magistrate who had extensive supervisory powers over the police and military. In May 1882 the Irish Chief Secretary and Under-Secretary were assassinated in Phoenix Park. The attack was carried out by the 'Invincibles', a republican splinter-group with close links to elements within the Land League. The government responded by establishing a new criminal investigation department. In September 1882 Edward Jenkinson selected seven officers to undertake special detective work and break up agrarian secret societies in the provinces.[32] Shortly after setting up this new detective force, Jenkinson met Waters in Westmeath, and in April 1883 he invited him to join it. Waters was posted to Sligo as Divisional District Inspector for the North-Western Division.[33] This was a turning-point in Waters career. He was to remain in the detective department for many years, and his memoir illuminates the inner workings of the Irish CID.

While Waters was stationed in Connacht he led another important criminal investigation, which the government considered second only in importance to the Phoenix Park case.[34] County Mayo was a stronghold of Fenianism and the birthplace of the Land League. Waters was sent there to investigate the activities of an agrarian secret society, allegedly led by the Mayo Land Leaguer Patrick W. Nally. The police believed he had conspired to murder a number of landlords in the Crossmolina district. In June 1883 Waters, acting upon the information of an informer named Andrew Coleman, arrested a number of suspects. The men were tried for conspiracy to murder, but the jury failed to reach a verdict, largely because the trial judge insisted that Coleman be regarded as an 'approver' rather than as an independent witness.[35] Waters therefore had to find evidence to corroborate the informer's testimony. This was a major problem in secret society cases because the danger to prosecution witnesses was considerable. He tracked down several independent witnesses and persuaded them to give evidence. He travelled to London to trace a young woman named Lizzie Clements, who had worked as a maid at Hughes's Hotel in Claremorris, where the conspirators had regularly met. A second trial in Cork in March 1884 resulted in Nally and six other men receiving long prison sentences.

Waters received two favourable records for his work on the Barbavilla and Crossmolina cases. In December 1883, after a brief spell as Divisional Crime Officer in Athlone, he was given responsibility for organising the Special Branch in Ulster. By this time Waters was regarded as a rising star, and in October 1885 he joined the headquarters staff as Jenkinson's private secretary. While Jenkinson was absent in London, directing the effort to suppress a Fenian bombing campaign, Waters had responsibility for the operation of the Special Branch throughout Ireland. During this time Waters pioneered the systematic collection and compilation of police intelligence on political organisations. He regularly obtained copies of the most advanced nationalist newspapers published in Ireland and extracted information for the government's use. He enabled the authorities to closely monitor National League activity and suppress any branches that appeared to practise intimidation.[36]

The failure of Home Rule and land purchase bills in June 1886 precipitated a resurgence of agrarian unrest in Ireland. The Conservative administration's response was initially sympathetic to the plight of the tenants. Waters recounts a journey to Kerry in September 1886 to brief the newly appointed Special Commissioner, Sir Redvers Buller, who was eager to mediate between landlords and tenants (pp. 61–2). However, in October 1886 the National League initiated the 'Plan of Campaign', a scheme to force landlords to reduce rents on selected estates. The Conservative government tried to suppress the Plan and in March 1887 appointed Arthur Balfour as Irish Chief Secretary. Towards the end of that year Balfour decided to create a special intelligence department to provide rapid information for the use of the Chief Secretary. Waters was selected to run this, and for the next four years he gathered intelligence on Irish political organisations and public figures. He carefully cross-referenced newspaper accounts of controversial incidents with police reports to point out inconsistencies and omissions that the Chief Secretary could use for political advantage in parliament.[37] Waters candidly remarks that he frequently provided 'spicy anecdotes, and racy comments on Irish current affairs and events, for the use of Unionist speakers from English platforms' (p. 63).

Arthur Balfour's employment of Irish civil officials for party political purposes remains a matter of historical controversy. The issue came to prominence when the government established a special parliamentary commission to investigate the Irish Parliamentary Party's involvement in the Land War.[38] Waters exposes the Unionist administration's complicity with *The Times* in their attempt to assail the personality of Irish political leaders. He records that police officers and Resident Magistrates secretly procured confidential information for the newspaper's solicitors to bolster their case against the Irish Party. He states that the government 'gave every assistance' to the newspaper in its case against Parnell (p. 67). Waters was ordered to supply *The Times*'s solicitors with useful information from the Special Branch records. However, when he expressed his disbelief in the allegations, the task was given to two Resident Magistrates, Alfred Horne and William Henry Joyce, both of whom were former RIC detectives. Joyce later claimed that Balfour was fully aware of what was going on and deliberately deceived the House of Commons by denying the government's direct connection with the *Times* case.[39] Public servants were legally bound to assist the commission by supplying any information, consistent with official secrecy, when called upon. Nevertheless, Waters's account demonstrates that the government did not behave impartially but systematically supplied confidential information to only one side in the dispute. The affair raised grave constitutional issues concerning the political neutrality of the civil service. The Unionist administration's employment of public officials on work altogether outside the scope of their legitimate duty remains a matter of historical debate.

Waters was ostracised for taking a sceptical view of the accusations made in *The Times*. However, he was rehabilitated when the case against Parnell collapsed in February 1889. Two months later he was promoted to County Inspector, and he continued as the Chief Secretary's intelligence officer until Balfour left Dublin Castle in November 1891. After Waters failed to secure an inheritance in Australia in 1892 he returned to Ireland for a spell of ordinary police duties as County Inspector of Kerry. The 1890s were relatively peaceful years during which Waters had time to enjoy family life and resume his association with the Harrington family. Waters first met Timothy and Edward Harrington in the mid-1870s when he was a junior officer in their home town of Castletown Bere-haven. He had enlisted their help to establish an amateur dramatic society in the town. Twenty years later the two brothers were both leading members of the National League and Parnellite MPs. It is remarkable that by 1896 the Harringtons' newspaper, the *Kerry Sentinel*, could publish flattering reports of theatrical performances by the County Inspector's children. In 1883 the newspaper had been temporarily closed down by the police for printing seditious material which cost Edward six months in jail. It indicates that relations between some nationalist politicians and the police changed significantly for the better after the bitter struggle of the Land War. It also demonstrates the ease with which Waters moved between the established and the new elites of Irish society.[40]

Waters returned to intelligence work as head of the Special Branch in 1898, and was promoted to Assistant Inspector-General in April 1901. He portrays the early twentieth century as a demoralising period for the RIC. He blamed a succession of weak political administrations for undermining the police's authority in the eyes of both nationalists and unionists, and for starving the police force of funds and curtailing its intelligence operations.[41] As a Protestant police officer who was proud of his Cromwellian ancestry, it is not surprising that Waters became involved in mainstream Unionist politics after he retired in 1906. He used his police contacts to collect information for propaganda on behalf of Walter Long's Union Defence League; he also edited the *Constabulary Gazette*. Waters briefly resumed intelligence work at

Dublin Castle following the Easter Rising in 1916. He returned in August 1919, before finally retiring from public duties following the assassination of his colleague Alan Bell by the IRA in March 1920.

Waters stayed in Dublin to weather the storm of the Anglo-Irish War and the Civil War as a private citizen. Despite occasionally losing the use of his car to a local unit of the IRA, he came through the conflict unscathed, which is perhaps remarkable for someone who had been so closely associated with those engaged in intelligence work. After the conflict was over Waters remained in Ireland and appears to have spent his final years in comfortable circumstances. He was supported by a generous police pension, having been the last RIC officer to retire on full pay. He and his wife, Helen, spent their final years at 'Woodview' in Stillorgan, and Waters had survived his wife by ten years when he died on 4 March 1936 aged eighty-nine. The Royal Irish Constabulary was disbanded in August 1922. However, Samuel Waters, one its most senior former officers, has left as a personal legacy this fascinating insight into what was, for a century, a central institution of Irish life.

Editorial Note

I have edited the original memoir of 34,000 words to 25,000 words, removing repetitive material relating to the author's sporting activities and material solely concerning family matters. I have placed short summaries of the deleted material, indicating the number of words used in the original typescript, at the appropriate places within the text. Otherwise I have intervened as little as possible in presenting the text. I have where necessary silently corrected minor spelling errors, but have retained original punctuation and capitalisations. Omissions of letters or words in the original typescript are indicated within square brackets.

Memoirs of Samuel A. W. Waters

[PRONI, Gore-Booth Papers, D/4051/14]

The history of my life — I wonder! Will it ever be written, and, if ever written, will it be worth reading? I doubt it. Here goes, however, to make a start; and, as it is meant only for the eyes of my children, and possibly grandchildren, I am sure of friendly critics anyhow.

All proper autobigraphies begin with the birth of the person concerned, so I shortly record that my dear mother introduced me into this world of care on the 20th October, 1846. My father was then an officer in the Irish Constabulary at the Depot in the Phoenix Park, and my mother was residing in rooms in a Dublin Street.

She was the daughter of a distinguished Dublin King's Counsel, father of the Bar on a Leinster circuit of Ireland [*sic*]. Late in life he retired and took Holy Orders, officiating in one of the Dublin Churches, where he died very suddenly in the Pulpit when delivering a sermon.

He was proud of his descent from George Walker[1] who closed the gates of Derry against the army of King James.

His wife, my grandmother, was leader of a fashion in Dublin Society; which, at the period, was as brilliant as in any country of Europe. My mother was the youngest of four daughters; and, when only sixteen years of age, she married Mr. Hardman who was heir to a good estate at Newbliss, in Co. Monaghan. There were two daughters only of this marriage — Mary and Fanny. Hardman was delicate, and died early of consumption at Pau in the South of France, leaving my mother a young widow with two little girls and a comfortable jointure to live on as long as she remained unmarried. She settled at Clontarf where my father was then stationed. They met, fell in love with each other and married. Rarely, I think, were two people joined together in matrimony who were so completely unsuited to each other. My father came from an old Cromwellian stock, and had much of the stern hard Puritan character. His training, such as it had been, was that of an Irish country village. He knew little of the world, and nothing at all of the habits and ways of the people amongst whom my mother's life had been spent. There was plenty of unhappiness in their married life but I leave it at that, as this is my history and not theirs.

My paternal grandfather, William Waters, was one of the first Chief Constables appointed in 1836, when Sir Robert Peel[2] reorganised the

Irish Police Forces, and established the system which practically remained unchanged until the RIC was disbanded in 1922. At the end of his days my grandfather fell into bad ways, and the Inspector-General of the day was anxious that he should retire from the force. My father was then about 18 years old, and Sir Duncan McGregor,[3] the Inspector-General referred to, sent for him and offered, if his father would retire at once, that he would appoint him a Cadet in his place. My father refused this offer, saying he would not be a party to putting compulsion on his parent. He said he would rather join up as a constable and take his chance of promotion in the ordinary course. Sir Duncan was pleased with this decision and promised my father he would keep an eye on him and would, if he did well, see that he was rapidly pushed forward. He kept his word so well that, in a very few years, my father was promoted to the rank of District Inspector.

I had two brothers, Richard and William and one sister Maud, all younger than myself. As I write Richard is still alive, but William, Maud, and my two step sisters have joined the great majority.

After my birth in 1846, my father was stationed at Ferbane in the King's County, but was very soon transferred to Carrick-on-Shannon, where all my early life was spent, and where I got all the education and youthful training that fell to my lot. The education was certainly fitful and erratic. Several schoolmasters succeeded each other in keeping a select academy for the sons of gentlemen. One, I remember, was an English clergyman who was always more or less the worse for drink. Another was a really clever teacher, from whom I learned all that was ever of much use to me. I forget even his name now; but one fine day he disappeared, having collected all his fees in advance and carrying off all our school books and property. He was heard of no more in Carrick-on-Shannon.

My father's brother, Sam Waters, was a remarkable character. He was a travelling agent of an English business firm and was married to a Scotch woman. They both lived their lives in a make-believe of extra gentility to which they had but a small claim. My Uncle Sam talked like a Merchant Prince, which he really persuaded himself, and tried to persuade us all, that he was. My Aunt boasted of her descent from the Campbells of Argyle. Her father was a Campbell, no doubt, but he kept a Hotel in Edinburgh, and, when my uncle met his future wife, she was helping in the bar! As his namesake, I always was a special pet of Uncle Sam, although I was not called after him, but after a paternal Uncle — The Rev. Samuel Abraham Walker, Rector of a parish near Bristol.

When I was about 11 years of age, I was sent to Edinburgh, where Uncle Sam resided. He placed me at a school where I was the only Irish student. There was one other boy who came from South America. All the other boys were Scotch; and, from the first, they put me into Coventry and made me the butt of the class at play hours, and, indeed, at all times. Naturally, I resented this; and I must say that, during the year I spent at this school, I learned nothing but mischief. The method for punishing there was with an instrument called a Taws, which consisted of a stout leather strap cut into strips. You held your hand and the leather came down and curled round your fingers in a particularly painful manner. Few days indeed passed that I did not get a taste of the taws, and I became so hardened to it that I hardly felt it at all in the end. I travelled all the way to Edinburgh and back by myself. In those days the train ran only to Longford, and the rest of the journey to Carrick was accomplished in a stage coach.

In those young days, most of my spare time was spent on the River. I learned to swim, to fish, to manage a boat with sail and oar and to shoot waterfowl of sorts in the reeds. I have sometimes thought, when looking back on these days, that I had so many escapes from serious accident, that I was meant to do some good in the world when I grew up. I recall one or two of these adventures which may be worth recording.

I was passionately fond of shooting, but my father strongly objected to my having a gun of my own. He possessed a small single barrel fowling piece — a muzzle loader of course. I used to sneak out with this weapon, having taken the barrel off the stock, which I hid under my coat. The barrel went down the leg of my trousers, and I limped out to a safe spot where I put the gun together and sought for something to shoot at. I was not very particular as to my game. I pursued water hens and baldcoots through the reeds, with an occasional lucky shot at a wild duck. If this failed, then thrushes and blackbirds became my victims. A favourite hunting ground for these poor birds was in a neighbouring garden which was reached by a very steep flight of stone steps. One day I was sitting on the top step with the gun on full cock on my knees, when it suddenly slipped from my grasp and went bumping down the steps with the muzzle pointed straight at my body. Back I went heels over head just as the gun went off, and the whole charge of shot whizzed past the soles of my boots as they were in the air.

I remember to the present moment, the horror of a position I got into as the result of a visit to a travelling circus. I was greatly taken with the exploits of an acrobat on a trapeze, particularly with his performance in hanging head downwards, holding on with his knees, and getting back with apparent ease. In our hay loft at home there were rafters across the roof and I decided to try this trick for myself.

I climbed up, got my legs over a rafter and let go, so that I hung head downwards. Never shall I forget my horror when I found it absolutely impossible to get back again. There was a drop to a hard floor of some eight or ten feet; but it looked to me like twenty. I screamed and yelled but no one came to me; and at last my legs gave way, and down I fell on my head to the floor, getting a terrible bruise but nothing worse.

My swimming saved my life at Rosses Point near Sligo, where we all went for sea bathing in the summer. The men's bathing place was on the sheltered side of the mouth of the river which ran up to Sligo. When there was an ebb tide a strong current ran round the point. I was bathing all alone as usual, and I struck out to sea boldly and swam on until I thought I heard a distant shout. I looked back to see the shore apparently flying away from me, and I realised I was being carried away by the tide. I turned about but could make no head way. Fortunately two priests, who were bathing a short way off, saw what had happened. They threw on some clothes and rushed back to the village where, with some difficulty, they got a boat and rowed out to me. I was picked up unconscious, just faintly paddling in the last extremity after over two hours of swimming! The local newspapers reported the rescue, and declared it was the prayers of the good priests alone that enabled me to hold out so long. Perhaps it was, but I fancy my hard training in the fresh water of the River Shannon had something to do with it.

Enough of my youthful adventures. I fear in my old age I am too much given to going back on these days.

When I was about fourteen years of age, my step sister Fanny became engaged to Tom Brereton who held a Commission in the Commisariat of those days. Fanny had a fortune in her own right of about £4,000 and my father insisted, with the strong approval of her guardian, Mr. Townley Hardman, that this should be setttled on herself and her children if any. Brereton objected to this, and demanded that the money should be used to pay off a mortgage on a small property he owned near Nenagh in Co. Tipperary. Fanny agreed with him, and my father refused to have anything to do with the wedding, so my mother and Fanny went off to Dublin where arrangements were made for the ceremony. I joined them and officiated in loco parentis by giving Fanny away. I recall that I was very proud of a fine new suit of clothes which were presented to me on the occasion. New suits of clothes were indeed rare with me! I thus left Carrick-on-Shannon, and it was some years before I saw it again.

My uncle, Sam Waters, wrote to my father that, if he would send me over to London, he would start me in business, and put me in the way to become a Merchant Prince like himself. My father agreed to this and to the great grief of my poor Mother, I was despatched to London. My uncle got me a billet as clerk in a firm of German ship brokers in Mark Lane, and I started my career there before I was fifteen years of age at the noble salary of twenty pounds a year. After a years experience with Messrs. Drelenvaux and Bremner I had got on so well that I became their chief shipping clerk. They were agents for a line of steamers from Hamburg to London; and my job was to clear from these vessels all goods for export abroad; and despatch them to their destination.

I thus became thoroughly familiar with the Custom House routine, and with all the London Docks and Warehouses. I left Drelenvaux and Bremner when I was sixteen and took a place as shipping clerk to a firm of Colonial exporters.[4] I held this until the firm became bankrupt and then, being nearly eighteen years of age, I determined to go back to Ireland and try to pass the examination for a cadetship in the Constabulary. I went to a Dublin grinder, and eventually passed with credit, taking first place of fifteen candidates, and making the second highest total of marks that had been recorded. The highest total had been made by a candidate who had been at the same grinding school with me and who passed in a couple of months before me. His name was Thomas Hartley Montgomery.[5] We were in the Depot together and when he left I lost sight of him for years. We met under tragic circumstances which I will relate later on. Montgomery had been a bank clerk and saved some money. When I met him at the Grinders he told me he had a small sum he wanted to invest. It happened before I left London that a friend of mine, who was a clerk in the office of one Albert Grant, a well known company promoter of the period, had told me that this man was preparing one of his greatest schemes, and had offered to get some of the original shares if I could raise the cash. This was quite hopeless to me and I had forgotten all about it until Montgomery spoke to me. I then told him about it and he asked me to write to my friend and try if I could still get the shares. I did so with the result that Montgomery got some shares in the 'Credit Foncier and Mobilier of France' which Grant had just floated. Later in my story I will show how this led to his ruin, to a terrible tragedy, and to his death on the scaffold. My six months at the Constabulary Depot passed over without incident worth recording. It was not in those days at all an admirable school for young men. Hard drinking was the fashion and the permanent officers in charge of the staff and recruits were all free livers and very thirsty souls. Mess Bills ran high and I left the Depot considerably in debt, partly for uniform and partly to moneylenders for cash advances to settle my mess bills.

I had at this time the princely income of £125 a year all told to keep myself and my horse. My first station was Grange in the County Sligo, a village half way between Sligo and Bundoran. I got lodgings with the post-mistress on very reasonable terms. My father sent me a young untrained horse which, with the help of my mounted orderly, I broke into saddle and harness in a very short time. This was in the year 1866 when the Fenian conspiracy was beginning to spread through the country. The mountain district around the Grange was full of young Fenian enthusiasts. They assembled at night for drills &c. and it was a great part of the duty of the Police to trace and disperse these gatherings. Fortunately they had no arms of any account and they never dreamed of facing a well equipped body of police. Their scouts gave the word if we approached near their meeting places and they forthwith broke up and dispersed.

I always loved outdoor sports and in Grange I devoted every spare hour, and I had plenty of time, to shooting, fishing and hunting. The great man of the district, Sir Robert Gore Booth[6] of Lissadell, kept a pack of harriers and a fine house always open to his friends in unbounded hospitality. He was always most kind to me. I had a room at my service whenever I wished to go there in the winter months and a horse from his stable to ride to the hounds. The family spent the summer at his London Residence. I almost invariably formed one of the party at his covert shoots and in walking the mountains after grouse. For fishing I kept a small boat on Lough Melvin near Bundoran, and many a happy hour I put in after salmon there. Kinlough, where I put up my horse when fishing the lake, was some twenty miles away. I used to leave home at 3 a.m., drive to Kinlough, getting there about 7 a.m., fish all day till dark and get back to Grange late at night. There was some river fishing also, specially on the River Bundrouse which runs from Lough Melvin to the sea, and took many a good salmon out of it.

The killing of my first big fish was rather an adventure. I was trolling for big trout in deep water when I hooked a fine salmon. I had him nearly exhausted when I saw a boat with two rowers starting out from the shore towards us. My boatman said

'I hope you have your salmon licence with you.'

'Salmon licence' I said. 'This is the first salmon I ever hooked and I never had a licence.'

'Then we had better break away, because those fellows are the water keepers and they will have you up.'

We were close to a small island. I fastened the rod to a twart and seized an oar.

'Pull away round the island' I said.

We soon got the island between us and the keepers and then I hauled in my fish, got him into the boat and away we went for the shore with the keeper in full pursuit.

We had a good start, however, and I jumped ashore, seized my fish, ran to my car and drove hot foot into Bundoran where I at once took out a licence — dated of course for that day. The next day I was again early on the lake and very soon the waterkeepers spotted me and came up.

'You killed a salmon here yesterday' said one of them in a very truculent voice.

'That's right' I said.

'Produce your licence.'

'Here you are' I replied, handing out my paper dated for the day before.

'What the Divil did you run away for?' asked the surprised official.

'Oh, just for fun. Good morning' and away went the bailiffs in very bad humour.

I was a keen cricketer in those days having been initiated in a small club when in London and I am fond of the game to the present hour. I started cricket wherever I went, if it was at all possible. I admit I never was any real good at the game. I was smart and active in the field, but never excelled with either bat or ball. At Grange, I set some of the young constables to work in a rough field. After a while a few civilians joined us, and I managed to get up a scratch eleven.

We got so pleased with our progress at the game that I challenged a team from a Regiment in Sligo to come out and play a match against us. A crowd of country folk assembled and we started the game, but, alas, the soldiers were too much for us and we got badly beaten. Of course cricket had never before been seen in or near Grange, and the crowd had no idea of how the game was going. Towards the end, however, I noticed a lot of stalwart young fellows collecting together at one end of the field. They were Fenians, every man of them, and I was rather uneasy. Suddenly one, who appeared to be a leader, came up and called me aside.

'They tell us, Sir, the soldiers are beating you.'

'It is too true I fear' I replied.

'Be Gor, we won't stand that' said he. 'There's a crowd of us here ready to back you, and, if you say the word, we'll belt the Divil out of them.'

I had great trouble in persuading him that it was only a friendly match and no ill feeling, but he went away very dissatisfied.

It was at this match that my old head constable,[7] who was acting as our umpire, distinguished himself by the following decisions. I was bowling, and I got a fairly straight ball which took the batsman on the leg.

'How's that?' I cried.

'OUT' said the head, and the soldier retired very unwillingly. Shortly after I got another chance, and again appealed.

'OUT' said the umpire without hesitation. Once more a ball hit a leg and I once more appealed. The head hesitated for a moment, then he whispered in my ear.

'Be Gor, Sir, I could not do it the third time' — then in a loud voice — 'NOT OUT.'

Enough of cricket at Grange. The head constable above mentioned was one of the old style of policemen. He knew very little drill, had only a hazy perception of the technical regulations of the Force, but he knew how to keep order in his sub-district, and it was a sight to see him separating combatants, or clearing out a public house at a fighting fair. Incidentally I may record here, that when he retired on pension, he opened a public house himself in Grange, and it was rumoured that he utilised his knowledge of the Licencing Laws to consistently break them whenever it suited his customers! He was, very unintentionally, the cause of my transfer in disgrace from Grange, as I presently will relate. He took all official care off my hands, did all my office work, kept all the accounts, and quite resented it if I proposed to do any office work. I was certainly a very ignorant young police officer. I had learned little or nothing at the Depot, and Lindley took good care I should learn very little at Grange. I remember once I suggested to him that I should study up the Code and Regulations, and get some knowledge of my duties.

'Oh, don't bother your head with them' said Lindley, 'It's time enough to study them when you are caught breaking one of them, and I'll mind that for you.'

Nemesis came, however, when I had been about three years in Grange, and Col. Hillier,[8] the then Deputy Inspector-General, arrived on inspection.

I was in bed, laid up with a broken collar bone, the result of a fall out hunting. Lindley received the inspecting officer at the present, with swords fixed to the carbines, which was quite contrary to regulation. Hillier was in very bad humour. He stared at the parade and said to Lindley: —

'Is this the way you have been taught to receive a superior officer?'

'Yes, Sir' said Lindley.

'Dismiss the parade, that will do' said Hillier turning away.

In those days Col. Sir John Stewart Wood,[9] the Inspector-General had issued a special memorandum on detective duties which all ranks were required to study carefully.[10] I had never even heard of it as Lindley had carefully put it aside as of no importance. Hillier called on the Head Constable to examine the men in their knowledge of this memorandum. He was speechless, and the men had never seen this document. Hillier called for the Inspection book and wrote this minute — 'This is the worst district I ever inspected. There is no drill known here and no police duties'!

The result was an unfavourable record for me and a transfer to the Co. Clare. To do poor Lindley justice he would have done anything to save me trouble, and this fiasco was a great blow to him.

On one occasion there was a hotly contested parliamentary election in progress at Sligo. I had got no orders up to the day before the polling so I thought I was quite safe in going off to spend the night with friends at Glenade, some twenty miles away, as they had a shooting party arranged for the next day. We had a merry night of it, and I was just getting into bed about one a.m., when a car drove up to the door. This turned out to be Lindley himself. A mounted orderly had arrived at 10 p.m., with orders for me to collect all my available force and arrive in Sligo for duty at six a.m. I had to dress hurriedly, pack up my traps, drive back to Grange, get into uniform, and go straight ahead to Sligo, where I was on duty in the streets, suppressing continuous riots, until the early hours of the following morning. I thought very little in these days of a night or two out of bed!

The winter of 1868 [*recte* 1867] was a very hard one. Snow fell heavily, and travelling by road was difficult and dangerous. We daily expected a rising of the Fenians. I slept always with a pistol under my pillow, and the men in the barracks next door with loaded carbines by their beds. We had arranged, in case of an outbreak, to retire on Lissadell which had been placed in a state of defence by Sir Robert. All windows were sandbagged and loopholed, guns mounted on the roof, and trees cut down round the house. Mounted patrols went out every night and co-operated with the police. These patrols were carried out by the grooms and stable attendants, and also by the male members of the family and by guests. A great friend of mine, Capt. Charles Wynne,[11] son-in-law of Sir Robert, always took his turn, accompanied by a guest, usually one Capt. Martin. The patrol of these two scouts invaribly led to Grange about midnight. They put their horses up in my stable and spent a night with me over a game of cards, with occasional refreshers of whiskey punch.

I often laughed to myself when I heard the ladies at Lissadell sympathising with them on the hardships they endured — out all night on horseback in such weather. Many a sly wink passed between Charley Wynne and me when this happened. He was a most cheery companion who had gone through the Crimean war from first to last and then to the Indian Mutiny. His tales of adventure were many and wonderful; and the marvel was that, in all his battles and skirmishes, he never got a wound. He had been in and out of the Redan, had led the forlorn hope at Delhi, and had been in hundreds of scraps without ever getting a scratch.[12]

He was a perpetual Grand Master of the Pig and Whistle Club at Lissadell, an institution which arose in this way. Sir Robert Gore Booth had a strong prejudice against smoking in the house. He would not allow it even in the Billiard Room, and there was no smoking room. When reasoned with about this he would say that smoking was only fit for servants and grooms; and if gentlemen chose to indulge in it at Lissadell they might go to the kitchen, where they would find congenial company. Charley Wynne took him at his word, and he instituted the Pig and Whistle Club, the members of which were any gentlemen residing in the house who wished to smoke before going to bed. The place of assembly was the large kitchen in the hours after the ladies had retired for the night. There was a great white wood table in the centre of the room; and when a new arrival turned up, he had to be initiated with the solemn rites as a Member of the Club, and was required to carve with his penknife on the table, a large tombstone, on which was recorded his name and the date of his initiation. The table in my time was pretty well covered with these carvings, amongst which were names of many distinguished men. Lissadell was infested with rats, and a common amusement in the Pig and Whistle Club was to destroy some of them in this fashion. Next to the kitchen range was large hot plate, in which there had worn a hole near the floor. Late at night rats used to continually pop in and out of this hole. The smokers used to make a pool by putting in a coin a-piece. Then each in turn took a large kitchen knife and stood beside the hole, holding the knife just over it. As a rat put its head out, down came the knife; and, with luck, the rat lost its head. The game was that each subscriber got five minutes with the knife and the one who killed the most rats took the pool.

[*Waters recounts the stories of a bird-shooting expedition at Cliffoney during which he was almost shot by his companion, Dr Carmichael, the Constabulary's medical attendant, and a hunt where he witnessed the death of a Mr Hanley, a veteran huntsman, who fell from his horse while riding with the Roscommon Fox Hounds at Frenchpark House, the residence of Lord De Freyne. He describes a subsequent encounter with his County Inspector, Timothy MacMaghon, while*

returning to duty in Grange on the train from Frenchpark two days late. The
County Inspector, being himself late back from leave took no action against him.
Circa 700 words]

The outbreak of the Fenian Conspiracy took place in the Spring of
1867. I have already referred to the drilling and preparations made by
the young men in the Sligo mountains. So serious had this become that,
at one time, the American Fenians had arranged to open a campaign in
the district; and, with this object, a vessel was chartered at New York,
laden with arms, and a number of Irish American officers who had
served in the Civil War between North and South, which had ended
not very long before this period. This vessel, named the 'Jacknell',
sailed for the Sligo Coast with the intention of landing the arms and
officers there; and they fully believed that a well organised army was
waiting to receive them. A certain Colonel Burke[13] was despatched to
Sligo some weeks before the ship was expected, to make all arrangements for her reception. This man arrived disguised as an English touring artist. He stopped at a hotel in Sligo, and there made acquaintance
with the Constabulary officer and the Resident Magistrate, with whom
he fraternised and became quite intimate.

He soon discovered that there was no army available, and that the
prospect of a successful rising in Sligo was quite hopeless. He therefore
decided to meet the Jacknell at sea and warn the officers on board that
the game was up. He hired a small sailing vessel on the excuse that he
was sketching coast scenery; and, in this boat, he spent his time sailing
in the Bay, waiting for the arrival of the American ship. He appeared in
my district at Mullaghmore, a small village on the coast near Cliffoney;
and, for a time, made this his headquarters with his boat. I interviewed
him there; but, as he had letters of introduction from the Sub-Inspector
at Sligo and from the Resident Magistrate, I did not interfere with him.

In due course the Jacknell turned up. He boarded her off the coast
and turned her back. Some of the crew objected to go to sea again as
provisions were running short, and there was a fight on board in which
two of the American Fenian officers were wounded. These men were

taken on shore at night and left lying on the beach, where they were discovered next morning by the Coast Guards, who at once sent for me, and I arrested them and had them conveyed to a hospital in Sligo. These were the first of the crew of the Jacknell who were made prisoners. The ship eventually sailed around the coast; and as provisions failed, the rest of the American officers were landed at Wexford, and were all made prisoners, tried and convicted.

The island of Innishmurray, which lies about six miles out in Sligo bay was the great headquarters of poteen makers. It was and indeed is still, as far as I know, a very interesting place. A pupil of St. Patrick, known as St. Mulasius, established a Monastery there, and many traces remain of the buildings put up by him. There are curious bee hive houses, and ancient tombs with many legends attached to them. In one of the houses there was a wooden image, which the islanders treated with much respect. They called it Father Mulash and they were very jealous of anyone interfering with it in any way. They tell a yarn that at one time a yacht came to anchor off the island and the sailors on board managed one night to steal Father Mulash and carry him off. When the yacht weighted anchor and sailed away a terrific storm arose. The sailor took fright and threw Father Mulash overboard. The storm at once went down and the image of the Saint was found next morning on the island and was reverently replaced in his shrine.

During the winter months the islanders were mainly employed in distilling poteen from grain supplied by the farmers on the mainland. The coast of Innishmurray is rock bound, and there was but one little inlet in which it was possible to beach or launch a boat without the help of the island people. A landing could only be effected in perfectly calm weather; and it was the duty of the coastguards to watch for a spell of frost, likely to keep the sea calm for a day or two, and then call upon me to furnish a force of police, which they conveyed to the island in one of their boats. We always left at an early hour of the morning and landed just at daybreak, when we searched the island thoroughly and invariably made considerable seizure of Stills, still heads, worms, wash, poteen and all the paraphernalia of the smugglers.

Once only we were caught by a sudden change of weather and had to spend ten days on the Island. We had landed a couple of days before Christmas, and we were thus compelled to spend the festive season as best we could among the islanders. We took possession of the school house; we commandeered a small rick of turf and kept up a good fire, over which we cooked such meals as we could secure. The islanders had for generations a Royal family of their own, to whom they paid a certain amount of respect. At the time I am writing about, they were governed by a queen, a very kindly old woman, who lent us a kettle, a frying pan and a saucepan; and, with these utensils, we did all our cooking. There were plenty of geese, ducks, and chickens to be had, and we chopped these up and fried them on the pan with potatoes. There were five Coastguards and four policemen beside myself. We all slept on the floor, and we had not our clothes off all the time. Of course, there was no chance of shaving; and, when the weather moderated sufficiently to launch the boat, we were a very bedraggled party as may be imagined.

The Queen had been very civil to us; and, in spite of law and order I left her quietly most of the illicit material which we had seized. She was so grateful that she asked me to taste a drop of a special brew of poteen which she reserved for herself and family. When I consented she produced a quart bottle from a secret hiding place and also an empty egg shell into which she poured a liberal tot of the spirit for my consumption. I asked her had she nothing but an egg shell to drink out of, and she told me the boys had had a dance in her house before Christmas; and, having too much drink, they fell out amongst themselves, had a free fight, and smashed every article of glass or crockery ware in the place!

[*The Goore-Booths were keen sailors, and while visiting the family in Grange, Waters became interested in sailing and took part in a yacht race at the annual Sligo Regatta on Lough Gill. Waters piloted a yacht of innovative but unstable design, and the vessel sank during the race. Waters also recalls the county balls he attended in Sligo and his encounter at one of them with a lady palmist who informed him that he would not live to the age of thirty.* Circa 700 words]

Shall I ever get away from Grange I wonder? So many reminiscences of these early days keep cropping up that I fear it is yielding to the garrulousness of old age to record much more of them.

Taking the risk I will tell of some spiritualistic experiences I had at Lissadell. When in London for the season, the Gore Booths had come across a wonderful medium called Holmes, who was, at this time, mystifying London with remarkable demonstrations of his power in calling up the spirits of the dead, and inducing them to make remarkable manifestations. They returned to Lissadell full of these experiences, and proceeded to hold seances in the hope of getting some exciting results. I joined in the proceedings, at first, I admit in a very incredulous frame of mind; but certainly things occurred which were very difficult to explain. We used to sit round a table in the dark with our fingers touching and forming a circle. Presently the table began to move up and down, and slight noises resembling taps, were heard. One of us asked if a spirit was there, and a tilt of the table was the reply in the affirmative. Then questions were asked, and replies received by calling out the alphabet, a tilt of the table, or a rap at a particular letter, eventually forming words and sentences. I may at once record the fact that never did we get from the spirits, if spirits they were, the smallest atom of information of the slightest use to any human being. Some of the replies were indeed ridiculous, and some absolutely false. As an illustration of this, I may mention one case in which Sir Robert was greatly interested. It may be remembered that I attended a contested election in Sligo, at which serious riots occured. During one of these Riots, a certain Captain King, a cousin of Sir Robert's, was shot dead, and Sir Robert was very anxious to know who had fired the fatal shot. It was generally believed, and I thought with reason, that the shot was accidentally fired by a companion of King's, who was holding his arm, while the mob pressed upon him, and who held a revolver in his other hand. Capt. King's friend, however, refused to accept this theory, and maintained that it was a deliberate murder.[14]

At our seances at Lissadell, Sir Robert always asked the spooks to help him trace out the murderer. The replies were invariably absurd. I suppose, in the course of half a dozen sittings, the spirits spelled out a dozen names of persons, not one of whom was near the scene when the tragedy occured. This rather choked off the Lissadell enthusiasts, and the seances died out.

Of adventures in poteen hunting, and in arresting Fenians, quelling riots etc., in the Grange district, I could fill pages, but I must get on to other scenes.

I arrived at Ballyvaughan, in the Co. Clare, at the end of the year 1870. I left the County Sligo with the worst possible record as a hopelessly ignorant police officer. My County Inspector in Sligo was an easy going old batchelor, who never bothered himself about his officers if all went well. He was a bit of a toady, and liked to get into good society, and loved a good dinner. I got him frequently invited to Lissadell, and, in return, he let me do much as I liked as to police duties. My new County Inspector in Clare was of very different type. Daniel Jennings[15] had reputation of being the sternest and most severe officer in the force. I remember well when he first inspected me, He was rather a small man with a fierce moustache, and a wicked eye. On parade, he looked me up and down from head to heel and back again, and, when the inspection was over, he took me to one side and gave me the worst dressing down I ever had in my life. He fairly put the heart across in me and left me determined to take his advice and learn my business. I owe it to him that I did there and then take seriously to the work of a police officer; and, during my time in Ballyvaughan, I worked hard, and laid the foundation of my career in the RIC, which was afterwards not without success. I may as well close the official story of my life at Ballyvaughan by recording the fact that, when I had been there about a year, I was again inspected by Col. Hillier. His minute on this occasion was to this effect 'I have now finished my inspection of Co. Clare. The force is in the highest possible condition, and the district of Ballyvaughan one of the best I have seen.'

I come now to the period of my life when I met my good wife. If I am, in this record, to tell the truth, the whole truth, and nothing but the truth, I must plead guilty to many flirtations. I fear I was very susceptible to the arrows of the winged God. As a boy in Carrick-on-Shannon I thought I was in love with one Anne Jane Scott, who was a huge girl, a head and shoulders over me, and a year or two older. She treated me with cold disdain. I know I tried to write sonnets to her, but I can only remember two lines, one of which ran as follows: —

> 'To me it brings no sorrow or pain
>
> To worship the features of lovely Anne Jane.'

When in London, I was deeply attached to [a] girl who, sad to say, threw me overboard, and married an old City man, who had plenty of money.

My flirtations never went beyond a sentimental attachment. Once only was I nearly caught in a tangle. While stationed at Grange, I met a very nice girl, who was stopping with some friends. We became very chummy; and, one day as we were alone in my friend's drawing room, she nestled up to me in such a way that I could not resist the temptation to kiss her. She threw her arms around me and said 'Oh! I am so glad we are engaged, but I fear my father will never consent.' I had not the least intention of being engaged, and I fervently prayed that her parent would prove obstinate, which he certainly did. He took her away forthwith, and from that day to this I have never seen or heard of her again.

At Ballyvaughan, my most intimate friend and companion in sport was John Christy, who resided at Ballyalliban, a short distance from the village. We went shooting and coursing together, and I also joined him in trapping various animals in the mountains. Foxes were very plentiful, and very destructive; and, as there were no foxhounds within fifty miles of miles of us, we used to trap these as vermin, and tan their skins to make rugs. One day, when wandering with my gun along the cliffs at Black Head on Galway Bay, I noticed, on a shelf of rock some distance down, traces of an otter den. Christy and I went there with a rope, and I was lowered down to the ledge, where I found unmistakable tracks of otters. We set traps there; and, in one week, we caught ten splendid animals whose skin made a beautiful fur. They then deserted the place, and we never got another.

I was always welcome to lunch or dinner at Ballyalliban; and one fine summer's day I rode up, as was my wont, about luncheon time. Mrs. Christy met me at the door and I told her I had heard she had a sister staying with her.

'Oh, yes' she said. 'I have, and she is fast asleep this moment on the sofa in the drawing room.'

I went into the room; and, on the sofa, covered with foxskin rugs was Miss Margaret Helen MacNab, who has now been my best of wives for over fifty years. She was the cheeriest and merriest of souls, full of life and energy, and we fell mutually in love with each other, almost at first sight. There were many troubles to face before and after we married; but we pulled through them all with great luck, and stuck to each other, through thick and thin, as we will, please God, for whatever few years may now be left to us.

I was transferred from Ballyvaughan to Cookstown in Co. Tyrone; and there I took a little house and furnished it. We were married at Castleconnel, Co. Limerick, on the 4th January 1872, and I took my bride back to Cookstown forthwith. I was but two years in Cookstown, and in these two years our first two children were born — Jane Edith Marian and Lucy Eleanor.

I have little to record of our life in Cookstown. It was a perfectly quiet and orderly district for ten months of the year; but, in the months of July and August, party feeling ran high and Protestants and Catholics were at each others throats by night and day. Drumming parties marched about, displaying orange or green symbols; and woe betide the party which dared to invade the territory of their opponents. Desperate riots took place; and the police were very helpless in face of hundreds of excited men, armed with rifles and revolvers. It was little use to bring the offenders before the local justice or before a Tyrone jury. The justices and the juries invariably disagreed. Protestants under no circumstances would convict Protestants, nor would Catholics convict their fellow religionists. Once August was passed, everything settled down, and Protestants and Catholics were good friends until the madness revived again the following year.

I have often thought that a good deal of the trouble which English politicians experienced in governing Ireland was due to the manner in which the Criminal law was administered in the North and in the South. The Criminal Law and Procedure Act[16] was in full force at the time I am writing of. Rioters in the South of Ireland were promptly brought before two Resident Magistrates, who dealt with them summarily. This procedure was never enforced in my time, though it afforded the only chance of bringing party rioters to justice.

While I am on the subject of party feeling in Ulster, I may as well relate an experience of mine, very many years later, when I was an Assistant Inspector-General. In the small town of Kilrea, in the Co. Londonderry, it had been the custom of the Orangemen to decorate the village pump with orange ribbons on the twelfth of July in each year.[17] The Catholics bitterly resented this; and, on the occasion I write of, they determined to decorate the pump with green ribbons on the fifteenth of August. The Orange-men announced that they would resist this to the last extremity; and I was sent to Kilrea, with a force of five hundred armed police to keep the peace between them. I had enough to do to keep the contending parties asunder.

It will be remembered that, in recording my life at the grinders and at the Depot, I told how I first met Thomas Hartley Montgomery, and the part I had taken in helping him to make a very successful gamble in some shares. It was with the utmost surprise and incredulity that I heard, on my arrival in Cookstown, that Montgomery was a prisoner in Omagh gaol, awaiting trial on a charge of having most brutally murdered a young bank clerk. I could not believe it possible that he was guilty, and I went to Omagh, and had an interview with him, in which, to my horror, he practically admitted his guilt, and pleaded that he was mad when he committed the deed. The callous and calculated brutality of the murder precluded all question of madness, and I left the gaol full of disgust, and never again saw the wretched man until I stood near him in Omagh Court House when he was condemned to death. The truth was that, inflamed probably by his first success, he went in heavily for gambling on the Stock Exchange; and at one time he had won a considerable sum of money. After a time luck turned against him, and he lost as persistently. At the time of the murder he was stationed at Newtown Stewart about ten miles from Omagh. He had incurred heavy liabilities to meet demands on shares, for which he was responsible; and he deliberately resolved to commit murder and robbery to obtain the money. He entered the local bank just as it closed for the day. Being a friend of the only clerk there, a young man named Glass, he was permitted to stay while he locked up the cash. When Glass turned towards the safe, Montgomery cut him down with a blow from a hedge slasher, which he had concealed up his sleeve. As the poor fellow lay on the floor, he knocked at him again and again and, finally, to make sure that he was dead, he took a paper file, and ran it into his brain through the ear. Montgomery helped himself to a couple of thousand pounds in notes and gold and walked quietly away. By a succession of fortunate circumstances, the crime was brought home to him; and he was hanged in the gaol at Omagh, and no murderer ever more thoroughly deserved his fate. I was ordered to take charge of the Court during his trial, and, as it was feared he might do something desperate if found guilty, I had to stand close to him with an armed guard, ready to overpower him if necessary.

Enough of Cookstown. I was transferred to Castletown Berehaven in 1874. It was a long and weary journey for the wife and the two little girls. Lucy was then only about 4 months old. We had a nurse with us, and our route lay through Cork, and thence to Dunmanway by rail. We had to travel 56 miles by road from Dunmanway to Castletown. We did this in a covered car, a vehicle almost unknown outside of Cork. We were a weary party when at last we reached our destination. I was at this time particularly hard up, a condition, I regret to say, not altogether unknown to me at other times! The furnishing of a little house at Berehaven was a serious question. We took lodgings at first, and very uncomfortable they were. I was always fond of carpentering, and I had brought a kit of tools with me. I found that timber of sorts was very plentiful and cheap, as quantities were constantly being washed up on the shore. A kindly resident made me a present of several logs of pine and hickory, which he cut into convenient boards and scantlings in his saw pit. Out of these I constructed sufficient furniture to start us in a small house, outside the town. Indeed I eventually made the entire furniture of the house, with the exception of a few cane chairs.

We were very much out of the world in those days. The only public conveyance was a small car, which ran between Castletown and Bantry. The district was absolutely peaceful. I could inspect all my stations in two days. We had a Petty Sessions Court once a month, and I felt badly treated if I got more than one official letter in a week. To me it was a paradise of sport. I had free shooting over twenty miles of bog and mountain. There were lakes and small rivers alive with trout. Grouse, woodcock, partridge, and snipe were plentiful. I was dissatisfied if I bagged less than twenty brace of snipe in a winter's day's walk. In summer, the lakes yielded me heavy baskets. One lake at Glenbeg so teemed with moderate sized fish that it was only a question of how many I wished to bring home. Fifteen dozen was an average take. I joined a young Doctor, George Armstrong, in running a 15 ton Galway hooker, which we had fitted with an otter trawl; and many a long day, and often a night as well, we spent out in Bantry Bay, trawling, or fishing with lines for gurnet or mackerel. We had also a lot of lobster pots, from which we took an ample supply of these fish. Berehaven was then, and indeed still is, a favourite station for the Channel Fleet, and the great excitement of the year was the arrival of the great War vessels in the Bay. I always called on the officers and we entertained them to the best of our ability and they responded most hospitably. Berehaven suited my limited means very well. Fish we always had in plenty for the catching of them. Fowl were also cheap; and, in summer, we were well supplied with excellent beef and mutton, fed on the mountains, at a cost of from 3d. to 4d. a pound. In winter we had little or no butcher's meat, but there was always plenty of game and sea fish.

I have already mentioned George Armstrong, my partner in the hooker. He became my most intimate friend in Berehaven. His father was our only local Justice of the Peace. A great object, which George and I always kept in view, was the chance of getting a criminal case sent for trial to Cork assizes. As I said before, there was a little or no crime committed in the district; but, when the country folk came into fair or market, and drank too much whisky, fights took place and occasionally a man was beaten. George was called in to fix up the wounded man; and, if he could stretch his conscience to declare his life in danger which he was well prepared to do, then we had a case of aggravated assault, causing grievous bodily harm, and old Dr. Armstrong, as a magistrate, promptly returned the case for trial at assizes. This meant a delightful trip at the public expense to Cork for George and me. How profitable it was may be guessed from the fact that we had 112 miles to drive to and from Dunmanway to catch the train to Cork, and this meant 112 ninepences to me,[18] and the same to George, in addition to what we could save out of liberal nightly allowances in Cork. I drove a strong pony which I then possessed, all the way to and from Dunmanway, where I left him with a brother officer till we returned. George of course accompanied me. He had pleasant friends in Cork who put us up free of expense, so that, after a high old time in the city, we came back with our pockets full [of] money. In this connection, however, the biggest haul we made was over a wreck, which occurred in a tremendous gale of wind. A sailing vessel, named the Cardross, had arrived in Cork from Central America, laden with timber. She was a rotten old ship, and leaked badly on the voyage. The crew mutinied in Cork, and refused to continue the journey to Liverpool, which was the vessel's proper destination. The Captain invoked the aid of the Cork magistrates, who compelled the crew to go on board, and the ship sailed once more, for the last time out of port. When well out at sea she encountered the full force of a South Westerly hurricane, which blew her clean out of her course; and eventually drove her on to the rocks within some ten miles of Castletown. The Captain, his wife, and all the crew save two seamen, were drowned, and the old ship broke into splinters which were scattered over the beach. On hearing of the disaster, George and I hurried to the scene; George to do what was possible for the ship wrecked mariners, and I to take statements from them of the facts of the case. At this time there was a great agitation in England to compel shipowners to be more careful in sending ships to sea in either an unfit condition, or badly overladen. Mr. Plimsoll[19] was the chief public character who took part in this agitiation. A brilliant idea struck me that here was a case for enquiry which might fetch George and myself even farther away than Cork. I wrote a lengthy statement direct to Mr. Plimsoll, who put the English Board of Trade into action; and, as a result, George and I were summoned to London to give evidence at an enquiry there.[20] I had collected from the wreckage a lot of the rottenest pieces of timber I could find — indeed they were plentiful enough. These I carried over to London; and, with them, and the evidence of the two sailors, the owners of the Cardross were mulcted in heavy penalties and costs. George and I had two trips to London on this job; and, as we put up with my Uncle Sam there, we made quite a little fortune out of it. When being cross-examined at the enquiry, by Counsel for the Defence of the shipowners, an amusing incident occurred, which caused laughter in Court. I was asked how I went to the scene of the wreck.

'I rode there' I replied.

'Oh! you rowed, did you? How far was it?'

'About ten miles.'

'Who went with you?'

'No one.'

'What sort of weather was it?'

'Very rough and stormy.'

'And do you tell us you rowed yourself for ten miles in a storm?'

'Yes, but I rode a horse!'

This was, by a long way, the most profitable wreck which occurred while I was in Castletown. There were many others in which life was lost, and it was the duty of the police to protect all property washed ashore. For this we were liberally paid by Lloyds Insurance people.[21]

The wife had a great friend in Castletown, a Mrs Ogilvy, whose husband was the Commanding Officer of Coast Guards. These two ladies played a trick on a wretched curate, against whom they had a grudge, which caused me some trouble. The man in question had come over from England to take a curacy at Adrigole, about ten miles from Castletown. He was certainly an objectionable prig, who looked upon us all as a sort of savages; and, occasionally, on Sunday evenings he lectured us from the pulpit on our misfortune in having to live in such a God forgotten country, thus being unable to realise the delights of London life to which he had been accustomed.

Some time before we arrived in Castletown, a Protestant Irish missionary preacher, who was employed to try to convert the Catholics, was found dead on the road side. The Protestants asserted that he had been murdered, but most people, with whom I agreed, believed that he had been accidently killed by a fall from his horse. The man's name was O'Rourke, and my good wife and Mrs. Ogilvy conceived the notable scheme of frightening the curate away by sending him a threatening letter. This document was drawn up by them secretly in a most blood thirsty manner. It was headed with a huge sketch of a skull and cross bones, and ordered the parson to quit the country forthwith, or he would get the fate of O'Rourke! What did the recipient do when the letter arrived, but post it direct to the Lord Lieutenant at Dublin Castle. In due time it was officially sent to me for enquiry and report. I had not, of course, the remotest idea that my wife was at the bottom of the affair. I strongly suspected that it was a bad practical joke, and I foresaw trouble if I could not get to the bottom of it. I told my wife of the difficulty and, after consultation with Mrs. Ogilvy, she told me the truth. My job now was to square the parson without giving the ladies away. I interviewed him and gave him my personal assurance that the letter was only a silly joke. He refused to accept this, and insisted on being told who was the author of the letter. I refused this, and I was able to satisfy the Inspector-General, in my report, that there was nothing serious in the business. The ladies were, I regret to say, not at all repentant; and were incensed at the demand for their names. They took revenge later on by playing on him the following most reprehensible practical joke. Among other complaints of his surroundings in Ireland, the curate frequently bemoaned his fate in never seeing a decent sweetmeat, of which he professed to be inordinately fond. On[e] Sunday, after the delivery of one of his objectionable sermons, he came in to supper with the Ogilvies. My good wife was there, and she saw, on Mrs. Ogilvy's dressing table, a box of medicated sweets, known as Tamar Indians. These tablets, which contained a powerful physic, were made up to represent very attractive chocolate creams.

The wife brought the box down and placed it on the table, where it soon caught the eye of the curate. He said 'What delightful looking sweets. I have seen nothing like them since I left England.' The box was passed over to him and he helped himself liberally to the contents. He had ten miles to ride home that night, and was so ill for days afterwards that he departed from the parish, and was seen no more in Castletown. I did not, of course, mind his sermons, or his priggishness, but I could never forgive him for slaughtering and devouring the only few thrushes and blackbirds that existed within miles of Adrigole. The only plantation district was round his house, and here a few poor birds had sheltered untouched for years. He borrowed a gun and shot them every one.

[*Waters recalls his wife's active participation in his hunting and fishing expeditions, which led to her being known by the local wits as 'the greatest sportswoman in Ireland'. He also describes another 'narrow escape from death' which he survived when his home-made pony trap went out of control and fell apart while descending a steep hill into Castletown. While careering through the town with only the axle of the trap to stand on, Waters was saved by the swift action of a road labourer who directed the pony into a ditch. Two of his daughters, Ethel and Maud, were born in Castletown. When Ethel was four years old she was taken to London for a year to live with her father's uncle Sam. Waters relates the hazardous journey the party made from Castletown to Bantry in a hooker during which, in thick fog and a heavy sea, they very nearly came to grief on the Rean Corrig in Bantry Bay.* Circa 1,400 words]

George Armstrong and I made many expeditions together; but the most interesting of these was an annual visit which we paid to the Bull Rock in quest of sea birds' eggs and large pollock. Three barren rocks rise high out of the Atlantic to the West of Dursey Island. They are known as the Bull, the Cow and the Calf. Of these the Calf lies about a mile from the Island's point, the Cow some four miles out, and the Bull, about seven miles. I believe the Bull is the bit of European land nearest to America. At the time I write of, the Bull Rock was the nesting place of thousands of sea fowl. Gannets, puffins, guillemots and all sorts of wild birds made their nests there, and reared their young, year after year. The rock could only be approached by a boat when the sea was perfectly calm. In the month of May we watched the barometer for a set of really fine weather; and then, having arranged beforehand to have a boat with six oarsmen ready at the Dursey Sound, we started from Castletown at 2 a.m., got to the boat quay at 3 a.m., and after a two hours row, reached the rock about 5.30. As we neared our destination, we could hear the sound of the various cries of the birds, blending together like the distant melody of a great band. When we landed on the rock, these birds kept flying round and round us quite close, and so thickly packed together, that a stone flung into the air was bound to hit one of them. The gannets were tame so that we had to kick them off their nests to secure their eggs. When we had secured a sufficient quantity of these, we took to the boat again and fished for pollock with lines which we had brought with us, baited with small eels. No sooner was the bait in the water than it was rushed at by several large fish, and we simply kept pulling them in, until we had as many as the boat could comfortably carry. Then away for home again. The crews of the boats which we hired for these trips were a very wild lot; and, on one occasion, they very nearly left us marooned on the rock. We always carried a basket of luncheon for ourselves and another for the crew. We brought a gallon jar full of draught beer for our own use, and some whiskey to divide amongst the rowers. On the day which I refer to we left the six men in charge of the boat and luncheon while we investigated the birds' nests. George always brought a gun with him, not to fire at the nesting birds, which we never did; but in case of getting a shot at some rare specimen on the way out or back. Luckily he had the gun on this particular occasion. We came back to the boat, both hungry and thirsty, to find that the crew had opened our jar of beer and drank it every drop. We lost our temper and went for the culprits with the strongest language in our vocabulary. The leader of the crew answered us in Irish; and, calling to the others, they all rushed into the boat, cast off, and were running away, when George presented the gun at them, shouting that if they did not instantly return he would shoot them dead. They stopped rowing, and then the leader called out that, if we said no more about the beer, they would take us in. Naturally we agreed to this, and they took us in, and back to Dursey Island. I remember we were parched with thirst, as, of course, there was no water on the rocks.

It was in Berehaven that I first made acquaintance with Timothy Harrington,[22] who afterwards became Secretary of the Land League, and a Member of Parliament. There never had been a theatrical performance in Castletown. I was always fond of acting and, as I had so little to do, I decided to get up a little play in the village school house. George Armstrong, myself and a young Bank Clerk formed the entire company. I made and painted the scenery; and we acted two small farces, which attracted a remarkably full house for two nights in succession. Before I had decided what to do with the scenery &c., I was approached by the Parish Priest, on behalf of the Roman Catholic Young Men's Debating Society, of which he was President. These young fellows were so taken by our performance that they became filled with ambition to produce dramatic pieces themselves. Timothy Harrington, then a lad of about seventeen years of age, was the leading spirit in the Debating Society; and he at once took the lead in the theatricals. I took a lot of trouble in coaching up the actors (there were no actresses) and, in particular, I taught Tim Harrington all I knew of stage craft and elocution. Years passed before I again met Harrington, under circumstances which will be detailed later on.

I left Berehaven on transfer to Lisnaskea in Co. Fermanagh in August 1877. I was in very poor health at the time, as I was only just recovering from a bad attack of typhoid fever, which left me more or less of a wreck for long enough. We had a very nice little cottage at Lisnsakea called Lisduff, and here we had a very uneventful time. Helen Gunning was born at Lisduff; and it was while we were at Lisnaskea, that I brought Edith back from London.

The County Inspector of Fermanagh at this time was Henry George Carey.[23] He is dead and gone long ago, and I will say as little as possible as to my official experiences while serving under him. He had the reputation of being a hard man over his officers, and had had many quarrels with them before I met him. He seemed to take a fancy to me while in Lisnaskea, and, when a vacancy occured in Enniskillen, he persuaded me to apply for it, promising to help me in many ways, particularly in regard to some extra pay and allowances, to which I might become entitled. With my increasing family the extra pay was a temptation, so I applied for the station and got it, as, indeed, no other officer could be found who would volunteer to serve under Mr. Carey. We got on pretty well at first; but very soon he turned against me; and from that out I had a very unhappy official life in Enniskillen. I made good and pleasant friends there who backed me up against the Co. Inspector, which naturally increased his animosity to me. Eventually he reported me to the Inspector-General on a long list of petty omissions which he had carefully collected from time to time. The Inspector-General of the day gave him no satisfaction, but his Private Secretary wrote to me offering me a transfer at public expense to Castlepollard in the County Westmeath. I took this offer, and soon we all migrated to the new station. Amy was born in Enniskillen, and was a very delicate baby, so much so indeed that we had her hurriedly christened in our Enniskillen abode. We had not even thought of a name for her when the clergyman asked for one. The wife suddenly remembered her Berehaven friend, Mrs. Ogilvy, whose name was Amy, and this was given to the infant. Once more I had to start afresh in a new station.

We settled in Lodgings for some months, and then got a nice little house, with a good garden, which we christened 'The Laurels'; and in this we spent all the time we were in Castlepollard. These were the early days of the Land League, and very soon after I took charge, its influence began to be felt in Westmeath. Agrarian outrages became frequent, rents were refused, evictions took place, and generally the County became seriously disturbed. Mr Forster[24] was then Chief Secretary, and what was known as the PP Act, i.e. the Protection of Life and Property Act,[25] was passed. The object of this law was to practically suspend the operation of the Habeas Corpus acts in Proclaimed districts in Ireland. Persons suspected of belonging to unlawful organisations could be arrested under the Lord Lieutenant's Warrant and detained in custody, without trial at his discretion. The idea was of course, to break up the criminal conspiracies which were at the bottom of all the terrorism which prevailed. There might have been some good result if the Act was sternly enforced. Mr. Forster was, however, a very kindly man, and he made such arrangements for the imprisonment of the suspects, that the special prisons set apart for them, were nothing more than fairly comfortable clubs, where the prisoners wanted for nothing but their liberty alone. Thus it happened that, so far from breaking up the conspiracies, the operation of the PP Act actually fostered them. If a prisoner did not belong to a secret organisation before he entered one of these special gaols, he was quickly enlisted there, and left a sworn member.

Mr. Forster's kindness was but little appreciated in Ireland, and he left the country a broken man. With a view to lessening the danger to life of firing bullets from the police carbines, he directed that cartridges filled with buckshot should be substituted, if it became necessary to have resort to fire arms in suppressing riots or dispersing unlawful meetings. Buckshot discharged from rifle barrels naturally scattered about far and wide, and one result of its use was that innocent persons, outside of the immediate area of disturbance, were frequently wounded. So far from appreciating the humane idea which led to the use of these missiles, the agitators declared that the object was to slaughter more of the people than could be effected by the bullet. They invented the epithet of 'Buckshot Forster' which stuck to the Chief Secretary and greatly irritated him. Mr. Forster had a Private Secretary[26] at this time who was of rather diminutive stature. He was dubbed 'Snipe Shot' much to his disgust.

Fenianism, as a military organisation, ceased to exist after the Rebellion of 1867. Michael Davitt,[27] and other leading spirits of the day, seeing the hopelessness of open armed resistance to England, conceived the idea of binding the people together in a great agitation, directed in the first instance against landlords, but with, of course, the ultimate aim of making it impossible to enforce British law in Ireland. Great numbers of the old Fenians joined in a secret organisation known as the Irish Republican Brotherhood. Beyond the avowed aim of this Body to secure by force of arms, if possible, the freedom of Ireland from British Rule, there was nothing absolutely criminal in the original idea of the IRB. When the land agitation spread through the country, however, a number of local secret societies arose, mostly formed and fostered by branches of the IRB. These conspirators arranged and carried out the murders and other desperate outrages which followed the track of the agitation wherever it appeared. It is no part of the scope of these memoirs, to dwell on the history of the Land League and its operations. I am concerned only in recording how far I was engaged in the performance of my police duties, in dealing with it in certain localities.

To return to my personal history — I took with me to Castlepollard a cob, which I picked up in a curious way while I was at Enniskillen; and which turned out one of the best and most profitable bits of horseflesh I ever possessed. It was one of my routine duties to attend a fair held in Blacklion, Co. Cavan, just over the borders of Fermanagh, and practically part of the village of Belcoo, which was in the latter County, and in my district. The railway line from Enniskillen to Sligo had just been opened as far as Belcoo; and, on one fair day, I went by train to this station, to take charge of the police on duty at the Fair. The last train back to Enniskillen left at 10 p.m., but, at this hour, I was engaged in clearing out a fighting mob in Blacklion, and I lost the train. I was thus left ten long miles from home, and no possible way of getting there save on my poor flat feet. As I was marching my party of police back to Belcoo, I saw a wretched looking country pony, equipped with saddle and bridle, standing outside a public house door. A brilliant idea struck me that I might borrow the beast to carry me home to Enniskillen. I found the owner in the public house, partly the worse for drink. I put my sergeant on to interview him, with the result that the owner refused to lend the animal, but offered to sell him, if I would then and there buy

him outright. After considerable trouble bargaining, I eventually
bought the animal for ten pounds, with the saddle thrown in for luck
penny. I rode home in triumph but I shall not soon forget the contempt
of my good wife when she saw my bargain in the stable next day. Truly
the pony was a miserable spectacle. Half-starved, ribs sticking out,
coated with mud, and in every way woebegone, it certainly seemed as
if I had paid dearly for my ten miles ride. With a little care, good feed-
ing and grooming, Puck soon showed his real quality, and a better little horse never ate oats. I bought a light trap to suit him in
Londonderry; and, for years, he was my stand-by in every emergency,
and never once failed me.

It may be remembered that I mentioned the name of Mr. Timothy
Harrington, as a young lad whom I had coached for his appearance on
the stage in Castletown Berehaven. He developed a remarkable gift of
eloquence; and, when the Land League was started, he took an active
part at meetings in Co. Cork, and soon became a very prominent character, so that he was soon elected as Secretary to the League, and took
up his domicile at the head-quarter office in Dublin. While I was in
Castlepollard he came to Mullingar to attend a meeting there. I was
present on duty in charge of a party of RIC. Harrington made a very
violent speech in which he advocated the non-payment of rents, and
the boycotting of obnoxious individuals. I reported the matter in due
course, and, as a result, a prosecution under the Crimes Act was instituted, and Tim was sent to prison for six months. While he was in gaol,
a vacancy occurred in Westmeath for a member of Parliament. Harrington was proposed and returned without opposition.[28] It was some
years afterwards that I met Tim on the terrace of the House of Commons. I had some doubt if he would recognise me, but, to my surprise,
he came up and shook me warmly by the hand.

'You have been one of my best friends' he said. 'You taught me how
to address an audience, and you sent me to gaol in Mullingar, and made
a member of Parliament of me!' Tim afterwards became Lord Mayor
of Dublin, where I frequently met him, and we were always the best of
friends.

I am now coming to incidents which gave me the opportunity, which by good luck, I seized, and which led to a complete change in my official career, and a very great improvement in my prospects of advancement in my profession. Many serious outrages had occurred in Westmeath; but, by far the most brutal, was the murder of Mrs. Henry Smyth [*recte* Smythe] in my district. She was the daughter-in-law [*recte* sister-in-law] of a Mr. Smyth, who was a large land owner residing at Barbavilla, near Collinstown. Mr. Smyth was a high handed old fashioned Tory landlord, who refused to give way in the smallest degree to the demands of his tenants for reduction of rents. He himself believed he was in danger, but he refused to have any police protection. On one Sunday morning, he drove in his close carriage, as was his habit, to the parish church. Mrs. Henry Smyth was staying in the house on a visit. The morning being fine, she walked to the church; but, after service, she took a seat home in the carriage. Mr. Smyth relinquished his usual seat in the back of the carriage to her, and sat in the front. As they drove through Barbavilla demesne, a charge of slugs was fired from behind a bush through the carriage window, taking poor Mrs. Smyth in the head, and literally blowing out her brains. I was on the spot within an hour of the occurence with all the police I could muster; but, though we searched for hours, no trace of the murderer could be found.

At this period, the Lord Lieutenant, had appointed Mr. Jenkinson[29] as his Assistant Under-Secretary for crime, with the object of establishing a more effective detective force to deal with the prevailing disorder. The country outside of Ulster was divided into two large districts, over each was placed a Divisional Commissioner, who was entrusted with large powers over the police and magistrates.[30] One of these Commissioners was stationed in Mullingar, and it was my duty to work under his orders in the effort to bring to justice the murderer of Mrs. Smyth. As a matter of fact, the man who fired the fatal shot was never caught. He escaped to America. We did, however, eventually lay bare the conspiracy which engineered the crime; and several of the conspirators were convicted, and sent to Penal Servitude.[31]

I had never met Mr. Jenkinson, and I knew little or nothing of the organisation of the new crime staff. One day as I was riding home from Collinstown on my good little Puck, I was cantering on the grass on the road side, swinging a polo stick as I was then keen on the game. I was in uniform, and a jaunting car came along with two passengers. One I at once recognised as a District Inspector of RIC. The car stopped as I came up. The other passenger was Mr. Jenkinson, and we had then and there a long talk over the murder case. Mr. Jenkinson entirely approved of all I had done; and he told me, if I had anything of interest to consult him about, I should run up to Dublin, to consult with him in person, which of course I was very pleased to do. Mr Jenkinson's Private Secretary was a Mr. Dunsterville,[32] a DI of the RIC. One day as I was waiting in his office to see the Asst. Under-Secretary, he told me there was a vacancy for a Divisional District Inspector at Sligo. I asked what sort of job it was, and if it was at all well paid. Dunsterville satisfied me on these points, and [I] forthwith made up my mind to have a try for the vacancy. At the end of our interview, I asked Jenkinson if he would recommend me for the appointment. He at once said he would be glad if I got it, but there were a number of senior officers on the list of applicants. Col. Bruce[33] was then our Inspector-General, a most kindly good-hearted fellow. Jenkinson advised me to see him at once; so I went straight to his office, got an interview, and made my request.

'But my dear Waters', said the IG. 'You are a married man with a family. Do you understand this will separate you from them for a long time?'

'I am quite prepared for that Sir.'

'Well, Colonel Forbes,[34] the Divisional Commissioner has already applied to have District Inspector Hayes[35] sent to him, and I have applications from about twenty other officers.'

'I fear, in that case, I am too late, and so it can't be helped.'

'I am not sure about that if you really want the job. As to Hayes, I would not permit him to go in any case for reasons of my own. I know there is [a] most important case pending in Mayo, which the new Divisional Officer must take up at once. I believe you are well suited for this work: and, as far as I am concerned, you may tell Mr. Jenkinson that you have my approval, and I wish you all good luck.'

We shook hands on that and I went back to Jenkinson and told him.

'All right' said he. 'Then you are appointed. I will send the formal notification tomorrow to Col. Forbes. Now I want you in Mayo as soon as you can possibly get there to take up the Crossmolina Conspiracy case which is nearly ripe for action. When can you start?'

'To-morrow morning, Sir, If you like. I can catch the night mail home, pack up my kit and be in Sligo to-morrow afternoon.'

'That's what I like' said Mr. Jenkinson. 'Off you go then. You will find all the papers in the office in Sligo; so set to work at once, and let me know from time to time how you get on.'

I was as good as my word, and I arrived in Sligo as I promised and reported myself to Col. Forbes, who was greatly surprised and annoyed that he had not got Mr. Hayes, whom he had selected. I afterwards found out that Hayes, very foolishly, had never applied to the Inspector-General for his approval of his appointment, and Col. Bruce was much offended by this oversight, and was therefore glad of the chance to pass him over and give the job to me. Poor Hayes got a very bad shock, as he had announced his departure to all his friends at his station in Donegal, and even given them a farewell dinner! Naturally, I had rather a bad time with Col. Forbes at first; but I was only a few days in Sligo when I departed for Ballina in Co. Mayo, where my most important work lay.

This Country had been greatly disturbed by the Land agitation. There had been several murders, in none of which had criminals been brought to justice. The local DI in Ballina had got hold of an informer,[36] who gave details of a widespread murder conspiracy, directed against certain landlords and agents in the Country. It was up to me to prevail on this man to give evidence in Court: and, if he agreed to do this, to collect sufficient corroboration of his story to convict the conspirators. I did prevail on the man to come forward, on a strict understanding that he would be protected, well rewarded, and sent out of the country when his work was done. I had to travel over all Mayo in quest of small items of evidence; and I succeeded in getting hold of some important witnesses in England. One I picked up, by a lucky accident, in a London public house. She had been a maid in a Claremorris [hotel], which was a favourite meeting place of the conspirators, and was able to tell of many conversations overheard by her, which were of great use in the prosecution.

To make a long story short, at three o'clock one summer's morning I had about twenty of the leading conspirators arrested at the same hour in various parts of the County. I myself took charge of the prime mover in the business; and eventually, in the City of Cork before a special jury, these men were convicted and sentenced to various terms of penal servitude.[37] The effect of the simultaneous arrests in Mayo was very remarkable. Within a week, there was a regular exodus of all the leading Secret Society men in the County. They fled to America in dozens; and for many years afterwards Mayo was one of the most peaceful Counties in Ireland. I have written at some length about this case as it was certainly the turning point in my career in the RIC. It was my start in the Crime Department; and I never again took up ordinary duty till I was appointed County Inspector of Kerry many years later on.

I was only about a year attached to the Sligo Division when it was broken up, and I was sent to Athlone, where an old friend Mr. Andrew Reed,[38] Assistant Inspector-General had been appointed Divisional Commissioner. All the time I was engaged in this way my good wife and the children remained at Castlepollard, where I visited them as often as I could get away. I thought I was fairly settled at Athlone for some time; and, accordingly, I took a very nice house there, had it done up, and even removed some of my furniture into it when I got another change. I had already arranged to take a house in Sligo, before I knew that I was going to Athlone, so that, at this time, I was actually tied down to three houses — one in Castlepollard, one in Sligo, and one in Athlone. The climax came when I was despatched to Armagh, where I had to take another house, thus having four on my hands in various parts of Ireland.

My work in Athlone was almost entirely in the office, and nothing occurred worth recording save perhaps the following escape I had after a silly night's gambling. My colleague in the Crime Department was a dear good fellow, DI Phillips.[39] He was a very delicate man who died not long after from consumption. We occupied a large double bedded room in lodgings and he was the best of a companion. When in Castlebar making up the evidence in the Crossmolina case, I had been very intimate with the officers of the Sherwood Foresters, then stationed there. The regiment had been transferred to Athlone, where I again met my friends. They asked Phillips and me to dine at mess one guest night, and of course we went.[40] The best of good cheer, and plenty of champagne, made me feel up for anything; and, when they suggested a round game of cards, I joined in at once without the least idea what the stakes might be. Phillips, who was very temperate and cautious, declined to play, and he looked on for a while. The game was unlimited loo, with a black force; and, as there were some 8 or 9 players, the pool soon mounted up to good round sums. Poor Phillips saw me losing steadily, and signing chits for considerable sums, which I lost as fast as I put them in. He got most uneasy, and whispered several times to me to give it up and come away. I refused to budge. At last he asked me if I had any idea of how much I had lost. I said something over £50.

'My God' he whispered. 'You are mad. I won't stay here to see this going on.' 'All right' I said, 'Go home and leave the door on the latch for me.'

Away he went, and I played on till about 3 a.m. Luck turned my way with a big run, and I got every one of my chits, and a bit beside.

I crept very quietly into our bedroom, so as not to disturb Phillips; but he was wide awake, and the moment I entered he said: – 'Well, tell me what happened. I have been most miserable about you.' 'Right as rain' said I. 'Got back all my chits and there's two pounds seventeen shillings and sixpence to the good.'

He leaped out of bed and danced round the room in the utmost delight.

Up to this period, the operations of the Crime Special Department, originated by Mr. Jenkinson, had never been extended to Ulster. He now decided to put in the edge of the wedge by sending up a crime special District Inspector to work in with the Ulster Officers in the establishment of a centralised detective department in the Northern Counties. It was a ticklish experiment as the Ulster officers were extremely jealous of the outside interference of a Divisional Commissioner, and were inclined to take it as a sort of slur on their own efficiency that any such department should be needed. The fact that I had served in Ulster, and, possibly, if I may say so, that I was generally popular with my brother officers, led Mr. Jenkinson to select me for this job. It was, of course, highly complimentary, and I could not think of refusing; but it was, as may be imagined, one more great upset. At this time Mr. Jenkinson, who had become Sir Edward Jenkinson, while retaining his position as Assistant Under-Secretary to the Lord Lieutenant, was specially employed at the Home Office in London, in assisting Scotland Yard to trace out the Irish Conspiracies which had caused much damage and alarm in England. I was allocated to Armagh, as the most central part of my district, which embraced the whole of Ulster; and, while I remained there for a period of two years; I was entirely a free agent at my work. I was responsible to no one but Sir Edward himself, to whom I reported direct, and no constabulary or other official in Ireland had any control over my movements.[41]

I found in Armagh, as County Inspector, my old friend Mr. Henry George Carey, under whom I had served with some discomfort in Enniskillen as I have already recorded. Times had indeed changed with us; and I am pleased to say that I found him changed very much for the better. We got on very well together, and had no friction at any time. I took a very comfortable house in Armagh, which had been the family residence of Sir William Kaye,[42] then an Assistant Under-Secretary in Dublin Castle. I managed to get rid of my three other houses and brought the wife and children to Abbey House.

[*Waters now had eight daughters and one son. Because of his wife's habit of dressing the six elder girls in sailor costumes, the children became known in Armagh as 'the Naval Brigade'. Waters recalled that William Reeves, the Bishop of Down and Connor, likened Abbey House to a verse in scripture, 'that in which*

it is recorded of a certain house that therein was the sound of many waters'.
While in Armagh, Waters continued to pursue his sporting activities, playing
cricket and tennis at the social club in the city, and gaining a reputation as a
first-class shot while hunting for snipe in the surrounding bogs and marshes.
Circa 600 words]

At the beginning of my career in Armagh, I visited all the Ulster
Counties in turn; interviewed the County Inspectors, explained the
objects and scope of the department, and prevailed upon them to
appoint special and selected constables to act upon my staff.[43] I am very
pleased to record that I never had the slightest disagreement with any
one of them. On the contrary, when I explained the full meaning and
objects of the new departure and its value, they rallied round me to a
man, and gave me every facility for my work.

When I had been about two years in Armagh, Sir Edward Jenkinson's Secretary, Dunsterville, whom I have mentioned before, was
appointed a Resident Magistrate. Jenkinson was still detained at the
Home Office in London, and Dunsterville acted for him in the Chief
Secretary's Office in Dublin Castle. I was offered Dunsterville's
vacancy; and of course I accepted it, and once more we migrated, this
time to Head Quarters. I took a house in Sandymount, named Towerville, with a nice garden, and here we settled for another brief
period. I did not remain long in the Chief Secretary's Office, as my
friend, Sir Edward Jenkinson, fell out with his colleague at the Home
Office, and retired into private life. The Crime Special Department
was then attached to the RIC, and I moved into the Constabulary office
in charge, under the Inspector-General.

It was while in the Chief Secretary's Office at this period that I first
made the acquaintance of Sir Redvers Buller,[44] who was then in charge
of Cork and Kerry as Divisional Commissioner. Serious crime was ram-
pant in Kerry, and the police had failed utterly in bringing criminals to
justice. One day, as I was writing in my room, I was sent for by Sir
Robert Hamilton,[45] who told me he had a most important despatch to
be conveyed forthwith to Sir Redvers, who was then in Killarney.

There were also some verbal instructions to be given by word of mouth only. He had selected me for to go on this mission; but it was essential I should catch the next train to the South, which left Kingsbridge in half an hour. I at once accepted the job; and, having got my instructions and my credentials, I called a car, drove to Kingsbridge, caught the train, and off to Killarney with only a light overcoat and no personal luggage whatever. I had just time to write a hurried line to the wife to be sent to her by special messenger. I arrived at Killarney just as Sir Redvers was sitting down to dinner at the hotel. I introduced myself, and explained the reason for my presence.

'Sit down and dine with me first' said he. 'The business can wait an hour or so longer.'

Sir Redvers was always given to good living, and hated to be disturbed at meals. After dinner, we had a long talk; and as he had no experience in Irish police matters, I was able to give him much general information, which he listened to with interest.[46]

He was a very broad minded man, and had already given offence to the extreme landlord, or rather Land Agent, class in Kerry by telling them plain truths about their treatment of tenantry. These gentlemen had been accustomed to look on the police as a sort of personal servants of their own, whose duty it was to back them up, no matter what they did. Sir Redvers very curtly let them know that the police had duties to perform, in the protection of the tenantry, just as important as in looking after the landlords. I intended, of course, to return to Dublin by the first train the next day; but Sir Redvers asked me to put in a week with his Secretary, Colonel Turner,[47] who was going on a tour round the South of the County, and who wanted a Police official to introduce him to the RIC, at the various stations we passed en route. I started on a jaunting car the next morning, with Col. Turner; being provided by Sir Redvers with a suit of pyjamas, a brush and comb, and a razor. We drove from Killarney to Glenbeigh, where there had been grave trouble over evictions. I knew the history of these evictions well from reading the official reports in the Castle, and I suggested to Col. Turner that he should call on the Parish Priest, who had taken a very active part on behalf of the tenants. We arrived at his house about eleven a.m., and were very well received. Before his reverence would enter into any conversation, he insisted on our having a tot of whiskey and soda. Turner was about to refuse, but I nudged him and whispered: — 'You will offend him if you refuse, and we will do no good.'

Accordingly we had our drink, and the priest became quite friendly and promised to give his utmost aid to Sir Redvers in restoring order in his parish. He kept his word, and Glenbeigh gave very little more trouble.[48]

We proceeded on our journey to Caherciveen, where we lunched. We then called on the Parish Priest there, and he produced a bottle of champagne, which we had to discuss before he would talk business. When we left his house, Turner said to me

'Look here, Waters, if this goes on I shall be drunk before we reach Kenmare!'

Fortunately, the persons we further interviewed were less hospitiable, and we got to our journey's end without disaster.

I spent a very pleasant week with Turner amongst the mountains and valleys of South Kerry, visiting police stations, protection posts, and many interesting people. I had no idea then that I should before very long be in charge of these stations as County Inspector.

Sir Redvers Buller was afterwards appointed Under-Secretary for Ireland; and I saw a good deal of him in the office. Colonel Turner was appointed Divisional Commissioner in his stead. I may say that neither of them was a great success. They were much too liberal in their ideas for the times; and were frequently hampered by the prejudices of the old fashioned magistrates and permanent officials. Sir Redvers was personally most popular. He entertained at the Under-Secretary's Lodge in a lavish style, which none of his predecessors could afford. His dinner parties, in particular, were the talk of Dublin society. When I met him in Killarney, he told me this story of his first experience of a special police sergeant. Shortly before his arrival, there had been a particularly shocking murder committed; and, as usual, there was no arrest, and no prospect of getting hold of the criminals.[49] He asked if there was not a special sergeant told off to investigate crime in the district, and was informed that a certain sergeant Smith held this position. He sent for Smith and this colloquy took place.

'Of course you know all about this murder, Sergeant?' asked Sir Redvers.

'I do well, Sir' replied the Sergeant.

'And you have, I hope, formed a theory as to it.'

'I have so Sir.'

'Well, out with it my man.'

'I know it to have been a most cold blooded and cruel crime Sir.'

'Oh, yes, but have you been trying to get information as to the murderers?'

'Oh, begorra, if I did that I could not live in the country at all.'

Sir Redvers fell back in dismay; and I need hardly say that Sergeant Smith did not enjoy his position as special sergeant much longer.

While I was in the Chief Secretary's Office I had an easy time of it; and had not enough work to fill my office hours. It was part of my business to look through the daily papers, and send on to Jenkinson any items of Irish news which might interest him in London. I enlarged this work by getting more papers from country districts, cutting out interesting paragraphs, and annotating them with the actual facts taken from official reports. Sir Robert Hamilton was then Under-Secretary and I showed him these extracts. He was greatly taken with the idea, and I always brought them to him to look over before sending them to London. This turned out to be of great advantage to me later on. I had only been a short time in charge at the RIC office when Mr. Arthur Balfour[50] was appointed Chief Secretary for Ireland. On his first visit to Dublin he consulted the Under-Secretary on the difficulty he experienced in Parliamentary debates, of having ready to his hand actual facts to at once meet false or exaggerated statements, made by Irish members. Sir Robert thought of my newspaper extracts. Mr. Balfour was taken with the idea, and he sent for me. We had a long talk together; and eventually I was asked to establish a special intelligence department for the information of the Chief Secretary. I was temporarily relieved from my police duties; and I got together a small staff, and set to work. I foresaw that, to reply to an Irish member by reading out an official report, would not be effective, as of course they would at once say these reports were cooked for the occasion. What I did was to watch all the Nationalist journals in all parts of the country for their reports of incidents, at all likely to be discussed by the Irish members in Parliament. I had these reports extracted and gummed on to sheets of foolscap. I then got the actual facts, and wrote them in opposite the extract. These papers were then carefully indexed by me and put away in convenient files for future reference. Whenever an Irish debate was expected, I was wired for to come over to London; and I crossed over, bringing my files and index books. During the debates, I sat with them in Mr. Balfour's private room in the House of Commons. If an Irish member made a statement, reflecting unfavourably on the action of an Irish official in any particular case, Mr. George Wyndham,[51] who was then Mr. Balfour's Secretary, would come round to me with a brief note. 'So and so has just attacked a certain Resident Magistrate, Police Officer, &c., and said he behaved in such a manner.' My memory was at this time particularly good, and I rarely had to refer to my indexes to identify the case. I got out my files, with a report, culled say, from the 'Freeman's Journal', giving a totally different account of the affair. Mr. Balfour was thus able to get up at once, refute the false account, and rub it in in a most effective manner, by reading out what the Hon. Member's own Journal had stated at the time of the occurrence, entirely at variance with the version given to the House. This proved most effective and entirely non-plussed the Irish Brigade.

Though the providing of rapid information to Mr. Balfour was the chief object of my Intelligence Department, it was by no means the only use to which it was applied. It was a frequent labour of mine to provide spicy anecdotes, and racy comments on Irish current affairs and events, for the use of Unionist speakers from English platforms. For instance, all the information on which was founded a series of letters to the English Press by Mr. George Wyndham, and which caused considerable sensation at the time, was furnished to him by me.[52]

Mr. Balfour's official Private Secretary was Mr. Thomas Browning, with whom I worked in the Irish Office on terms of closest intimacy and friendship. Poor Tom Browning! He was in wretched health, and suffered agonies from rheumatism and sciatica, but he never failed at his work. Often he lay for a whole day on a sofa, hardly able to move, but still working away, dictating correspondence, or going over the Parliamentary work with me. The Irish Solicitor General was Mr. Madden,[53] afterwards a distinguished judge. It was part of my job to coach him up in all matters likely to be touched on in debate. He was a very cheery soul, and never failed to greet me when I turned up in his room, with the cry 'Hallo! Stormy Petrel! here you are again. Now we are in for a row!' He took great interest in my family; and never failed to ask how all the youngsters were getting on. In this he differed from Mr. Balfour, as I discovered to my dismay in this fashion.

On one occasion, when a question arose, as to some extra remuneration for my work, Tom Browning thought he would enlist Mr. Balfour's sympathy by telling him what a large family I had to support. Mr. Balfour turned on him and said,

'I am sorry you told me this, Browning. It lowers my good opinion of Waters. I thought he was a man of common sense. He had no business to have such a large family. I consider it most improvident of him.'

Work at the Irish Office was indeed strenuous in these days. Browning and I began at 10 a.m., and worked till 8 p.m., when we adjourned for dinner. Then back to the House of Commons at 10 p.m. and it was quite common to be kept there till 2 or 3 a.m. Browning broke down at last, and lived but a short time to enjoy a good billet, which he secured as a Commissioner of Inland Revenue.

It has always been a matter of great self congratulation that I only once, in all the time that I was connected with Mr. Balfour, gave him away by a wrong tip. He never liked Mr. Trevelyan,[54] whose manner to him in the House was always irritating. One night when I was very weary, Mr. Wyndham came down with a statement made by Trevelyan for me to verify. I thought I knew all about it, and sent up a reply, which was incorrect. Next morning, on reading the Debate in the 'Times' I saw what I had done; and I at once went to Mr. Balfour, and told him I had badly let him down. 'Don't say it was to Trevelyan, Waters' said he. 'Alas! Sir,' I replied, 'it is too true, it was in reply to him the error occurred.'

'Well, I wish it had been to anyone else, but it can't be helped. Tell me all about it, and I will apologise in the House this evening.'

I was very much downcast that evening until Mr. Balfour came into the room all smiles.

'It is all right, Waters' he said. 'Your mistake has done no harm at all. I apologised to Trevelyan; and for the first time in my experience he behaved like a perfect gentleman, and I have had a most refreshing surprise.'

The success of Mr. Balfour's regime in Ireland is a matter of history. He ruled with an iron hand, but always it was covered with a velvet glove. He never deserted an Irish official who did his duty. He dealt with disturbers of the peace, and outrage mongers with consistent sterness; but, at the same time, he developed industries, opened new facilities for inland trade and commerce, and specially aided the peasantry of the West and South with large grants of money for important public works. The pity of it was that his example was not followed by his successors, and, with weak vacillating government, things in Ireland soon fell back into the old groove.

It is easy to moralise on the mistakes which successive Lord Lieutenants and Chief Secretaries made in attempting to combat the national antagonism to England. One tried to kill this sentiment by coercion and force, another by conciliation and yielding, bit by bit, to the popular feeling. It is possible that either of these policies might have had success if carried out to the end, and accompanied by wise and generous legislation in aid of Irish needs.

As a matter of fact, the frequent changes of political parties in England was the great curse of Irish Government. Each Chief Secretary came with a plan of his own to settle the country; but each one did little more than disorganise the system established by his predecessor, when he too had to give way to a new man with a new scheme. I firmly believe that if Ireland, immediately after Mr. Balfour's term of office, had been constituted a Crown Colony, with a permanent Governor, for choice a capable Irishman, and an Executive Council also independent of British politics, the country would have settled down to peaceful industries, and all the calamities of recent years would have been avoided.

This is a digression from my own history, which, after all, was what I set out to write; but, as I recall these days, when I was behind the scenes, and had particular opportunites of seeing how things were managed, it is not easy to avoid some comment on them.

Our family, when we settled in Towerville, consisted of nine daughters and one son. Arthur was born in Towerville, where we lived for a year or so, when we changed to a larger house in Park Avenue quite close by. Dick and Olive were born there, which completed our contribution to the population of ten daughters and three sons. There was another son born in Castlepollard; but he did not survive his birth, owing no doubt to a drunken doctor's neglect.[55]

[*Faced with the prospect of supporting a large number of daughters with only limited means, Waters sought to provide them with an opportunity of earning their own living, thus enabling them to avoid, for a time at least, the 'marriage market'. With the help of George Wyndham's wife, the Countess of Grosvenor, Waters secured employment for his three eldest daughters at Mrs Kerr's ladies' hat shop in Duke Street, Dublin.* Circa 400 words]

It was while I was engaged in charge of Mr. Balfour's Irish Intelligence Department that a commission was issued to investigate the truth of certain statements published in the London 'Times' accusing the Irish Parliamentary Party of direct complicity in the crimes which resulted from the Land League conspiracy in Ireland. Mr. Charles Stewart Parnell[56] was then the leader of the Irish Nationalists, and the articles were specially directed against him, as being personally responsible for the outrages. The 'Times' articles were founded upon information supplied by a Dublin journalist named Pigott;[57] and, though the

Government of day repudiated all responsibility for the truth or false-hood of the charges made, they undoubtedly believed, as the Editor of the 'Times' did, that they were well founded, and they gave every assistance to the 'Times' in the endeavour to bring them home to the persons accused. As I still continued in charge of the Crime Special records in Dublin Castle, I was required to go through these papers and supply to the Counsel for the 'Times' all the information which I could extract which might be of use. I may say here that I never believed in the stories told by Pigott; and I could find nothing in the records which could be used in support of the allegations. I reported to this effect, but my statements were discredited, and I was required to hand over my records to a Mr. Horne,[58] a Resident Magistrate who, as a Constabulary Officer, had a reputation as a clever detective. The entire expense of this commission was borne by the 'Times' and it was enormous. Police officers, magistrates, landlords &c. by the dozen, were summoned to London to give evidence; and no doubt details of many gruesome tragedies were given in the witness box, and the responsibility of the Land League for most of these crimes was proved beyond question. It was another matter, however, to bring home direct responsibility for the crimes to Mr. Parnell or any of his Parliamentary subordinates. The evidence of Pigott was broken down on cross-examination. The whole case collapsed, and Mr. Parnell came out unscathed. I was summoned as a witness; but, in view of my report, and the fact that I was totally incredulous as to the soundness of Pigott's statements, I was never examined. I remember well that I was in the beginning given the cold shoulder very unpleasantly by my colleagues in the Irish Office who firmly believed in the 'Times' and its statements. When all was over, I need hardly say I was congratulated on my attitude; and a very high official indeed expressed his regret that the Government had not acted on my report. The whole story is, of course, a matter of history, as is the fate of the informer Pigott, who came to an untimely end very soon after the collapse of his case.[59]

While this commission lasted, London was full of Irish witnesses, who were all lodged in first class hotels and highly paid by the 'Times'. A number of RIC officers resided temporarily in the Primrose Club, off St. James' Street. I took up my quarters there also, renewed acquaintance with many old friends, and enjoyed many cheery nights in their company.

I think it is very probable that I was one of the oldest cyclists in Ireland. In the year 1866, I purchased a bone shaker bicycle which a blacksmith in Sligo had put together on a pattern brought back from an Exhibition in Paris. This machine had wooden wheels shod with iron. It was driven by a simple crank on the front wheel; and on a level road it was quite possible to get up a speed of 8 to 10 miles an hour. It could not be driven up any sort of a hill; and a journey of say 15 miles gave one quite enough for the day. I rode all sorts of bicycles and tricycles from time to time, and I only mention them here because, when we were living in Sandymount, we had seven tricycles of sorts, on which the wife and I, with seven daughters, used to parade the roads on summer evenings. Violet was a tiny tot at this time and she had a little tricycle to fit her. I got a bad fright one day which I still remember. Violet and I had ridden to Killiney, near Kingstown, and we started to descend a very steep hill, which led down to the sea shore. Suddenly the brake on Violet's little machine gave way, and off she went down the hill at a terrific pace, and disappeared round a corner. I followed as fast as I dared, fearing greatly to find the child dashed to pieces; but, to my great relief, I found her at the bottom of the hill, sitting on the road side perfectly unconcerned, and the tricycle smashed up beside her. When the safety bicycles were introduced, Violet became a very expert rider, and used to entertain us with all sorts of tricks.

Shortly after the collapse of the 'Times' enquiry, I was specially promoted to the rank of County Inspector; and, when Mr. Balfour decided to retire from the Irish Chief Secretaryship, I went back to the Castle, in the belief that I could again take up my work in the Crime Special Department. Sir Andrew Reed, the Inspector-General, had, in my absence, nominated District Inspector Gibbons[60] as my locum tenens, and I fully understood that, when Mr. Balfour ceased to require my services, I should resume my old position. I was so confident that I was permanently settled in Dublin, that I had purchased the lease of a nice residence in Blackrock. Sir Andrew, however, decided that I should take charge of a County, and resume work as an ordinary officer of the Force. It was Mr. Balfour's desire that I should be promoted to the rank of Assistant Inspector-General, but Sir Andrew refused to permit this, and I fear that it was this well meant interference of Mr. Balfour's that led the Inspector-General to order me out of the Headquarter Office.

The County Inspector of Kerry had applied for a transfer from that County to a smaller one, as he found the work too severe. I was offered either a small County or Kerry. I chose the latter and was ordered there in due course. I left the family at Whitehall while I went to Tralee to take charge of the County Force. I lived for a time in lodgings, looking out for a suitable house. I then took a furnished mansion as a temporary measure, until a very nice place called Ballyard became vacant; and eventually we all settled there.

Mountain scenery had always a very great attraction for me. I loved the mountains in Berehaven, and I was never happier than when I tramped through the heather with dog and gun. On my first tour of inspection in Kerry I was charmed with the wild scenery of the South and West of the County. While on the staff in Dublin, I had few opportunities of taking out a gun, and now I looked forward to having some good sport. As I approached the village of Anniscaul on the Dingle penninsula, I saw large tracts of marshy bog, which looked to me ideal for snipe shooting. I asked the sergeant at Anniscaul if the game was preserved and he told me there was a large tract of country, which had been purchased by tenants, who permitted anyone to shoot over it. I found there was a guide in the village who, at times, went with some officers from Tralee; and I at once got hold of this fellow, and arranged a day to come again and bring my gun. I did so, and had my first experience of a Kerry gamekeeper in this fashion. We had tramped over some miles of bog, with varying success, getting a snipe here, and there, as we went along, when, suddenly, we arrived in a particularly nice looking swamp, in which the snipe were very plentiful. I was banging away, when I heard a shout, and saw an old man coming down the hill towards us, waving his hands in the air.

'Who is this?' I asked my gilly.

'Oh! It's only the gamekeeper' said he.

'The gamekeeper But I told you not to bring me on any preserved land. Who is the landlord?'

'Lord Cork;[61] but sure he has never been here in his life.'

I was very much annoyed, and went to meet the man and accosted him in my best manner.

'I am extremely sorry I have been trespassing. I had no idea I was on Lord Cork's property, but I will write to him and tell him how well you are looking after the game.'

The old man did not reply, but looked at me in a very surprised fashion. I turned away with my guide and as we left he said 'That's the biggest suck-in that fellow has had in his life. Sure he only wanted half a crown, and you might shoot as long as you like!'

I happened to know Lord Cork's agent, and, when I got home, I wrote to him, explaining the incident and apologising. I got a very nice reply, with a written permission to shoot over the Anniscaul property. I went there again shortly after, met my friend the gamekeeper, and this time I gratified him with his half crown tip.

Irish gamekeepers and waterkeepers were sometimes a queer lot. As an instance of their perception of their duties in protecting salmon fisheries, I may tell this incident. My step-sister, Fanny Brereton, resided at Rathurles near Nenagh in Co. Tipperary. A tributary of the Shannon ran through the demesne; and, quite close to the house, there was a pool, to which salmon regularly came to spawn in the winter. These fish were constantly poached by the neighbouring peasants. My sister one day met one of the local fishery conservators in Nenagh and told him about the pool. He asked if she would mind if he sent a man to stop the poaching. Of course she had no objection; and next day a water bailiff turned up, and spent his day watching the river. My sister saw him in the morning and told him to drop in to the kitchen for his dinner, which he did and was hospitably entertained by the cook. When he was leaving at night he came to her, and, pulling a big fish full of spawn from under his coat, he slapped it on to the kitchen table and said: — 'You have been so decent to me that I just brought you in this fish for the Missis's dinner.'

I come now to an event which opened with a brilliant prospect but which ended in disaster. My father had a younger brother who emigrated to Australia as a youth and joined the New South Wales Police. He had an adventurous career in his earlier days in pursuit of bushrangers and other criminals, and evetually rose to a good position in the Force and when he retired on pension, he settled in the town of Bathurst. He never married, and we always understood that he had accumulated considerable wealth. He took a prominent part in local affairs at Bathurst and had been Mayor of that town. Shortly after I was ordered to Kerry, I got a letter from Mr. Hulks in Bathurst, informing me that my uncle was dead and that I was left his heir. He said there was a considerable property to be looked after, and he advised me to come out at once and take possession. Naturally, our hopes ran high, and I decided to start forthwith at once. I had at this time, wonderful to say, a good balance to my credit at my bankers so, putting a hundred pounds in my pocket, and getting two months leave of absence, I went to London, took a return ticket to Sidney, and embarked at Tilbury on the good ship Orient.

We had a delightful passage out, and I thoroughly enjoyed every hour of it. I made great friends with the ship's officers, and with some members of the theatrical company who were on their way for an Australian tour. We had the usual concerts, dances and theatrical entertainments. I had provided myself with a book called the 'Orient Guide',[62] which gave full particulars of all places of interest which we passed or called at. I always read up in the book these particulars before we reached a port or passed any special spot. Thus I was able to tell my fellow passengers all about them; and I got to be recognised as a wonderful guide. There was a woman on board who attracted the attention of all the male passengers and the envy of all the females. She was a Mrs. Henry and was travelling in great style with her husband. A splendid looking woman, full life of life and energy, who took a leading part in all our amusements. When the ship reached Melbourne, she went

ashore with her husband, and we parted with her with much regret.
We stayed a day and night at Melbourne; and, of course, we all went
ashore and inspected the City. I was with a small party of three or four
men; and, feeling thirsty, we entered a restaurant in one of the principal streets. When at the bar I looked round and, to my surprise, I saw
Mrs. Henry leaning over the counter and chatting with one of the bar-
maids. I asked the girl who was serving us, who the barmaid was, and
she replied 'She is a Miss Slavin, sister of the great boxer, and that's
another sister talking to her, who has just come out from England.'

When we returned to the ship and related this adventure, much was
the glee of the ladies, and the discomfiture of the men who had made
so much of the fair lady on the voyage out.

It was in Melbourne on this same day that I had a rather remarkable
experience. I was, in company with my companions, crossing one of
the main streets, when a hand was placed on my shoulder, and, on looking round, I saw a stalwart looking fellow with a huge black beard who
said: – 'Surely, your name is Waters, and you were once a police officer in Cookstown.'

'That's me' I replied.

'Of course you don't recognise me.'

'Well, I must confess I don't.'

'Do you remember a boy, the son of a Presbyterian Minister, who
lived next door to you, and whom you often took out for drives in your
dog cart?'

'I do well' I said. 'But surely you are not him.' 'Indeed I am' he
replied 'and I knew you the minute I saw you.'

I reached Bathurst in due course, and interviewed Mr. Hulks, who,
I found, was acting as executor to my uncle's will. Here I met with
nothing but disappointment. The will, instead of leaving me the only
heir, left all the property equally divided between me and my two
brothers. On enquiring what the property consisted of, I found that all
the ready capital had been invested by my uncle in some mushroom
land banks which had been started in Sydney a year or so before he
died. These banks had offered interest on deposits of ten and twelve

per cent; and my unfortunate uncle was so bitten by these high rates that he realised almost everything he possessed, and invested in these deposits. A short time before he died, these banks began to collapse; and one after another became insolvent, and he lost nearly all his capital in them. When I reached Bathurst, there were still one or two holding out, and they had about one thousand pounds on deposit. This money, however, could not be claimed for several months, and meantime, the banks were extremely shaky, and it was pretty evident there was little hope of getting anything out of them. My uncle had left a little over £100 in his current account in the local bank, and there were several houses and some land in Bathurst which had been his property. As the result, partly of the bank failures, and general depression in the country, it was not possible to sell these houses or land at the time, and there was nothing for it but to give a power of attorney to a local Solicitor to act for me when times got better, and all I got, when I started for home again, was one hundred sovereigns from the local bank account. I may close this story of my Australian fortune by recording the fact that all I ever got from the attorney at Bathurst, as he sold the property, was a regular supply of bills of costs, and a very few pounds in cash. Of course I was well robbed, but I could do nothing. The worst of it was that, believing we were going to be full of money, we went ahead a bit in our expenditure, and I had nothing but worries and anxieties as the result. I must say that I found the people in Bathurst most hospitable; and if I had accepted all the invitations to stay with different people, I might have spent months there free of expense for living. The Mayor at the time was a shopkeeper, who was an Irishman. When I was introduced to him, he took me into his private office and showed me a hogshead of Jameson's whiskey, which he regularly imported from Dublin for his own consumption, and we had a drink together, of course.

To go back in my record, I may here mention [a] little incident which occurred in London, as I was going through on my outward journey. I had called at the Irish office and had a chat with my old friends there. Mr. Balfour came in, and I told him I was off in quest of my fortune.

He looked at me rather oddly and said, 'Tell me, Waters, did you know of this inheritance when you were having your big family?'

It struck me at once that what he had in his mind was what he had said to Browning, about my improvidence, which I have already related.

'Well', I said 'Of course I knew it would drop in some time or other.'

'I am glad to hear that' said he. 'That certainly made a difference. I wish you the best of good luck' and he shook me warmly by the hand.

On the voyage home from Sydney the ship called at Hobart Town, the capital of Tasmania. My old friend, Sir Robert Hamilton, who had been Under-Secretary in Dublin Castle in the days of Mr. Balfour, was then Governor of the Colony.[63] I wrote to Lady Hamilton from Sydney, saying I was passing by, and would have a day to spend at Hobart Town, and asking if I might call to see her. When the ship arrived at the Wharf, an Aide de Camp came on board, and asked for me. He took me up to Government House, where I lunched with the Hamiltons. Lady Hamilton asked me to dine with them in the evening, and go to the theatre, where a London company was playing. On looking at the playbill, I was surprised to find that the play was one written by an old friend of mine in my young days in London, and that he and his wife were taking the leading parts. Between the Acts I sent my name in to Jack Dodds and I was conducted behind the scenes to his wife's dressing room where we had a chat and a drink. I went behind again when the play was over, and as a result I very nearly lost my ship. She was timed to leave at eleven thirty p.m. and in the middle of a pleasant gossip with the Dodds I looked at my watch to find it was a quarter past eleven. I said a hurried good-bye, rushed out of the theatre, fortunately caught a passing cab, drove to the wharf, and just jumped on board as the last gangway was being hauled in.

I was elected as president of the Amusement Committee on the way home, and we were a very merry party. The night before we arrived in London, some of the passengers entertained me to dinner at the Holborn Restaurant. We had a cheery night of it, and parted swearing eternal friendship with each other. Alas! I have never met one of them since.

My wife, Edith and Lucy, met me in London on my arrival there on my way home. I had a pocket full of Australian sovereigns to show them as an earnest of the fortune and we spent a pleasant day or two in London, and then went back to Whitehall, and soon on to Kerry where we settled for a time at Belmont.

In a narrow lane which ran from the public road alongside Belmont there was a wretched tumble-down cottage, in which resided a poor crippled woman and three children, two girls and a boy. Amy, in her walks with the governess, discovered this family in great poverty and at once took them in charge. She got a comfortable arm chair for the woman, clothes for the children, and brought them food regularly. Years afterwards, when Amy was married to the best of husbands, she did not forget the poor woman in the lane, and when she died she took charge of the children and provided well for their future.

I bought a smart little pony in Cork which Amy used to ride and it turned out a capital bargain. We had him all the time we were in Kerry and took him to Dublin where the wife regularly drove him in a smart trap. When we were leaving Kerry we had an outdoor servant named Quinlan and we decided to take him with us. He was left behind to come on after us and bring the pony. He had never before left home and he was rather frightened at the idea. He started with the pony from Tralee, but at Kilkenny his heart failed him, and he got out intending to go home. Fortunately, one of my men who was at the station, recognised and asked him what he was about. When he heard that he had the pony in [his] charge and was about to forsake it, he took him by arm, and flung him into the horse-box, and so he came to Dublin all right. Denis Quinlan stayed with us at Convent House, and never returned to Kerry.

Ballyard House, which I eventually settled in, was a very comfortable mansion, at a moderate rent, which included the shooting over a large tract of mountain.

The Kerry folk were very genial and most kind and hospitable to us in every way. Tralee was a very cheery place in these days. There was a garrison at the military barracks, and the officers became great friends of ours. There was plenty of cricket and tennis in summer. There was shooting and constant dances, theatricals and other entertainments in the winter. The Land League troubles had passed away, and during the six years I spent in Kerry, the County was perfectly peaceful.

The Police were favourites everywhere with the people. I started annual police sports at Tralee, and got the band down from Dublin to perform to them year after year. The country folk came in thousands to witness these sports; and I always realised a good round sum, which went to a charitable fund for needy widows and orphans of the men of the RIC.

We held these sports in an enclosed field which was rented by the Gaelic Athletic Association for hurling and football. I paid them a rent for the use of this field for our sports, and also as a ground for the RIC Cricket Club, which I had established. Of course, the Gaelic Athelic Association was an ultra Nationalist organisation; but there never was any ill feeling between them and the police. We did not interfere with them in their hurling or football contests, which often enough ended in a free fight, and many broken heads, and in return, they backed up our sports heartily. The leading Nationalist paper in Tralee — 'The Kerry Sentinel' — was edited by Edward Harrington,[64] brother of Tim Harrington, already mentioned in this record. I am sorry to record that Ned was a thirsty soul, who paid little attention to his business. He was, however, blessed with an excellent wife, who practically did all the editing that was to be done. Mrs. Harrington was a great admirer of our family; and she devoted a good deal of space in the 'Sentinel' to the doings of the Waters family. I quote here a few extracts as samples of this kindly feeling. This from the 'Sentinel' of 12th September, 1896.

'A very successful concert, in connection with the RIC Cricket and Athletic Club, came off on Tuesday evening at the Garrison theatre at Ballymullen . . . The troupe of children, trained by Miss Amy Waters, went through their admirable Gipsy Dance . . . The children again delighted everyone with a pretty Spanish Dance, into which was introduced a pas de quarte, by Misses Violet Waters, Cecile Waters, Lillie Watchorn and Lillie O'Toole, which was a tremendous success. Little Miss Olive Waters, a tot of six years old, was the premiere danseuse, and performed a pas de seul in the most charming manner. Miss Violet Waters had a most brilliant success as a street ballad singer . . . She was loudly encored and presented with a lovely bouquet.'

It was while we were in Kerry that we first made the acquaintance of Walter Johnstone,[65] Ralph's brother, who was then a Captain in the Royal Irish Regiment stationed, as well as I remember, at Portumna in Galway. He came on a visit to Ballyard, and I remember he told me he had never shot a woodcock in his life. I took him off to my shoot in Foley's Glen; and, sure enough with the aid of my good dog Jorum, we found a cock which he shot to his great delight. Walter became a very frequent and welcome visitor. He was a great man at cricket; and he used to play for the RIC Team in matches, and the men were always delighted with the way he slogged the ball all over the field. He helped us to win many a good match. He was my companion on many a day on the Kerry Mountains, in pursuit of game, and many a good bag we made together. One year I rented a very fine mountain near Castleisland from Lord Ventry, and Walter and I did very well on it. The gamekeeper on this shoot was something of a character. He had given offence in the days of the Land League, and his life was threatened, so that it became necessary to establish a special post of two policemen to protect him.[66]

This post still continued while I was in Kerry; and, of course, the fact that I had always two of my own men always with him, did something to keep him up to the mark in preserving the game. He always expected a liberal supply of whiskey when out with the guns; and, if he did not get it, he took care that the sport was poor. I remember that I once gave leave to two officers in Tralee to have a day out with him, and they were horribly disappointed when they got little for their day but hard walking over the roughest of ground. When I next met the old keeper, I asked him how it was that these officers got so little sport.

'Is it them?' said he. 'They were the manest poor crathures I had ever anything to do with. What do you think they brought out in the way of drink? A bottle of porter, Morryah? Is it let the like of them shoot your game? The Divil a fear of me.'

I have dwelt a good deal on my shooting experiences in Kerry, which were, on the whole, very satisfactory. I have always been a very keen fisherman; and, on my first tour round the County, I was delighted with the look of the many rivers and streams, seemingly the most perfect haunts for trout and salmon. Alas, these rivers were mostly frauds. The country people were born poachers; and they systematically cleared out the pools of trout and salmon, with nets, spurge, spears and lime. I had occasionally some good white trout fishing, and, at Castlegregory, there was a shallow lake, which afforded good sport in the early season for brown trout. The lake was about a mile long, and half a mile across; and, at no part, was more than a few feet deep. I established a sort of small fishing club, consisting of ten members only. We hired a small cottage on the lake shore, which consisted of two rooms only, — a kitchen and a large bedroom, in which we placed two small bedsteads. A flat bottom boat completed the outfit; and, in May and June, we took it in turns, two at a time to spend a few nights at this cottage and fish the lake.

It was in Kerry I first took up golf. The Crosbies of Ardfert, had a private links on the sea shore; and here I took my first lessons in the game. At Castlegregory, there was a stretch of sandhills, with perfect turf here and there, which made an ideal natural course. I started a golf club in Tralee, and we used to make excursions to Castlegregory, and play on a rough natural course which I laid out there. Golf went ahead very soon in Kerry, and, before I left, there was a nice grass links at Killarney, and a very sporting sea side course at Dooks near Glenbeigh.

When I had been about three years settled in Ballyard, I had a serious disagreement with the Divisional Commissioner in Cork as to certain police matters, in which I thought he was unduly interfering with my authority. I was led to believe that I would be transferred to another County. I was not altogether dissatisfied with this prospect, as I had, for some time, found that we were going a bit too fast, and I was getting into debt once more. I decided to break up the Ballyard establishment; and, as a preliminary measure, I sent the wife, and all the family, except my daughter Maud, up to Blackrock near Dublin, where they took rooms in a terrace opposite the sea shore.

[*While the family were lodging at Idrone Terrace in Blackrock, Waters's seven-year-old son contracted a near-fatal attack of blood-poisoning which left him physically handicapped. While nursing the boy, his daughter Lucy became engaged to her future husband.* Circa 100 words]

I sold off my furniture by auction at Ballyard, and Maud and I took lodgings in Tralee, while I awaited my orders for transfer. At this time, Mr. John Morley[67] was Chief Secretary, and his Private Secretary was an old friend of mine, Mr. Lawrence Dowdall,[68] who had been the Chief Clerk at the Irish office when I was working for Mr. Arthur Balfour. When the file of papers from the Divisional Commissioner, came up suggesting my transfer, Sir Andrew Reed, the Inspector-General, submitted it to Mr. Morley, recommending that I should be moved, as it was evident that I was not getting on with Capt. Stokes.[69] My friend Dowdall spoke up for me to the Chief Secretary, who was always a very honest straight-forward official; and the result was that he returned the papers to Sir Andrew Reed with a minute, stating that, in his opinion, if anyone deserved to be transferred, it was Capt. Stokes and not me, as I seemed to have been entirely in the right, and Capt. Stokes in the wrong! It ended in Capt. Stokes asking me to go to Cork and talk over matters with him; and we became good friends once more, and it was settled that I should remain in Kerry.

The trouble now was to find a new house in which to settle the family, and here I fell on my feet once more. Robert Fitzgerald, an intimate friend, was agent to the Chute Family, whose mansion, Chute Hall, was then vacant. This was a fine old house, standing in a demesne, some three miles from Tralee, and was fairly comfortably furnished. Fitzgerald was anxious to get a safe tenant who would keep the house aired; and he offered it to me at the rent of £5 a month. There was no other house then vacant, and I got special permission to occupy Chute Hall on the condition that, if a suitable house became vacant in Tralee, I should move into it. I got back the wife and family from Blackrock, and we settled down in Chute Hall. It was indeed a cheap and pleasant domicile.

[*While at Chute Hall, Waters and his wife celebrated their silver wedding anniversary. During the family's six years in Kerry his six eldest daughters met their future husbands. Ethel married George Noble in London, Nellie married Walter Johnstone, and Edith married his brother Ralph. Lucy married Dick Maunsell, and Florence met her future husband Claud Hughes. Amy married Hedworth Grogan, who died shortly afterwards, leaving her a widow at nineteen years of age. She later married George Noble's brother John. Maud became engaged to Captain Arthur Scott, but soon broke off the engagement.* Circa 1,000 words]

We were a very merry and happy family at this time, and the girls had lots of friends, male and female, who visited us and kept the old house lively. We had three happy years in Chute Hall, and then, unfortunately, a house became vacant at Blennerville, a suburb of Tralee, and I felt bound by the terms of my permission to live so far out, to take this house, which I did. We furnished it up, and once more shifted our quarters. We were there but a very short time when I was offered the position of Chief of the Crime Special Department at the Castle. Of course I accepted, and I was accordingly transferred to Dublin, to once more take up duties on the staff. We left Kerry with great regret; and my kind friends there presented me with a very flattering address, and a handsome testimonial when I parted from them. This address was the fourth I had received in the course of my service in Irish country districts. I received one when leaving Grange, Enniskillen, and Castlepollard.

[*On his return to Dublin, Waters moved into Convent House in Clontarf, so as to be able to indulge his new-found enthusiasm for golf at the nearby Royal Dublin Golf Links.* Circa 300 words]

Sir Andrew Reed was still Inspector-General when I left Kerry. But, shortly after I arrived in Dublin, his time came round to retire on pension. He reported to Government that he was ready to retire whenever it suited the Lord Lieutenant to fill the vacancy. It was decided to offer the appointment once more to an army officer; and, as Lord Wolseley[70] was then in South Africa, a communication was sent to him asking if he could suggest a suitable superior officer for the post. Lord Wolseley, had on his staff as his Military Secretary, Colonel Neville Chamberlain;[71] and on getting the notification, he forthwith appointed Col. Chamberlain as Inspector-General, without any further reference to [the] authorities, either English or Irish. The first intimation we had of it in the RIC Office was appearance of a paragraph in the 'Irish Times' that Colonel Chamberlain had been so appointed. I saw the announcement when I arrived in the office, the morning it appeared, and I at once took it in to Sir Andrew, who was very much surprised, as it was the first he had heard of the matter. In due course Col. Chamberlain arrived, and took over charge. The new Inspector-General was, in every way, a most charming fellow. He made friends with every one, and we were all only too pleased to work under such a genial chief. To me, in particular, he was always most friendly, and we worked together, while I remained in the Force, in the most perfect harmony. Shortly after he took charge, a vacancy occurred for an Assistant Inspector-General, and, on his recommendation, I was promoted to this rank, which I held till I retired.

With the advent of a Conservative Government in 1903, my old friend Mr. Arthur Balfour became Prime Minister, and another old friend Mr. George Wyndham, came to Ireland as Chief Secretary.[72] No official ever took that uncertain position with brighter prospects. The Wyndham Land Purchase Act,[73] which he had piloted through Parliament, was a most popular measure; and its author secured lots of friends in Ireland to welcome his arrival. He started well, following the lines of his former Chief, by maintaining the power of law, while he dealt sympathetically with the real grievances of the people. I think there can be no doubt that this popularity led him astray in the end. He fell into the hands of certain sentimental Nationalists, who flattered him on his family connection with Lord Edward Fitzgerald,[74] of '98 fame, and he came to believe that he could really rule Ireland by working on the Nationalist sentiment, and do this without maintaining the strict police rule of his predecessors. He appointed, as his Under-Secretary,

Sir Antony MacDonnell,[75] an Irishman, who had a distinguished career in India, but who had no experience at all of the condition of affairs in Ireland. Sir Antony had special influence with the Irish Roman Catholic hierarchy and priesthood; and he relied more on the information and advice he received from them, and from other Nationalist leaders, than on the official reports of the police and magistrates. In this way, and at this period, was begun that interference with the influence of the police and magistrates, which eventually ended in the disasters of later years. It is rather sad to reflect that the thin edge of the wedge, driven in afterwards by radical governments, was first inserted under a strictly Unionist regime. My colleague in the RIC office, and my most intimate friend, was Heffernan Considine,[76] who was appointed Deputy Inspector-General on the retirement of Sir Henry Thynne[77] in 1900. Mr. Considine had been a Resident Magistrate, and he undoubtedly owed his appointment to the fact that he was a Roman Catholic. As the Inspector-General, and the three Assistant Inspectors-Generals, were Protestants, it was considered that the second in command should be of the persuasion of the great majority of the rank and file of the Force. Let me hasten to record the fact that Heffernan Considine never, for a moment, allowed the question of religious feeling to affect, in the slightest degree, his official acts. He was a most scrupulous Catholic in his attention to all the claims of his Church; but he resented as a gross insult, any attempt, by priests or others, to influence him in the discharge of his public duties by an appeal to religion. A more perfect gentleman never lived, nor one who was animated by higher principles of justice and right. His special department in the RIC office was to deal with crime and matters affecting the peace of the country, and in this I was his right hand man. He deplored, as much as I did, the attitude of Sir Antony, but we had no influence with him. Sir Antony was really a kindly man in private life, but he had a very hot temper; and, as a result probably of his Indian training, he could not stand any opposition to his preconceived opinions. Thus, if he got from the Crime Special Department a report as to the operations and spread in the country of secret organisations, he simply treated it with contempt, and refused to credit it. Many a time he sent for me when he got such a report; and if I attempted to support the sources of our information, he would dance round the room in a rage, and exclaim 'D–n it all, Waters! you and your Crime Special staff have got conspiracies on the brain. I don't believe a word of it!'[78]

Enough of these days in office. Col. Chamberlain had received the honour of a Civil CB, as the result of the visit of King Edward to Ireland.[79] He interfered very little indeed in the Crime Department, leaving it all to Considine and me. He took great interest in the police arrangements for the protection of the King and Queen, and in these matters I was fully employed also. Amongst other places visited by the Royal Party, was the City of Kilkenny, where they stayed for a couple of days with the Marquis of Ormonde.[80] The County Inspector had reported that there was a very bad feeling amongst the extreme nationalists in Kilkenny, and he feared there would be trouble when the Royal Party arrived. The majority of the Town Council were extreme Nationalists, and they had decided, if the King came, to invite a well known agitator named Daly,[81] from Limerick to visit the city at the same time, and bring with him a large contingent of Limerick roughs. The County Inspector believed it would require a very large force, both of military and police, to keep order, and ensure the safety of the King and Queen. I was despatched to Kilkenny some days before the date arranged for the visit to see what could be done, and to make all the necessary arrangements. I had an interview with the County Inspector who was very pessimistic. I asked him if he had consulted with the Mayor and local Justices. To my surprise, he told me he did not know who the Mayor was! In any case, he assured me, it was perfectly hopeless to expect any help from him, as he was certain to be one of the extreme faction. I found out that the Mayor was a stonecutter in the City,[82] and I decided to call on him, much against the opinion of the County Inspector. I found his worship in his shop, engaged in his trade, and he came to meet me looking very much surprised. I told him who I was, and assured him I considered it my first duty to consult with him, as the first magistrate in the City, and that I was more anxious that the police should work in with him and the local Justices, in preventing any unseemly demonstrations on the occasion of the King's visit. He was greatly flattered and he said: —

'Well Sir, you are the first police official who has ever approached me on anything connected with the peace of the City; and now I may tell you that, if you had not come to me there would have been trouble, but you may rely on me to do all in my power to put a stop to it.'

I pointed out to him that unless I was fully assured that the King would be treated with respect, and that there would be no fear of disturbance, it would be my duty to bring in an overwhelming force of police and military, the cost of which would fall on the City. He asked me to wait till the next day before doing anything, as he intended to call a special meeting of the Town Council for that evening, and consult with them. The next day he saw me early in the morning and told me the Council were so pleased with my action that they guaranteed that not a word would be said against the King, if I did not put them to the expense of a large force. They telegraphed to Daly in Limerick not to come to Kilkenny. I took the risk of only ordering a small force of the County constabulary, and everything went off most satisfactorily. The King and Queen were received with perfect respect and no untoward incident occurred. I had the honour of being personally presented to their Majesties, and congratulated on the success of my arrangements. Lord Ormonde was very uneasy indeed, and very doubtful of the wisdom of my action. He wanted to have a couple of regiments and a battery of artillery brought in; but he yielded to my strong protests, and was very pleased when all went well. So far as I was concerned the Royal visit resulted in a medal, which of [course required a] full dress uniform, which the King himself designed as a special honour for the superior officers of the Force, but which I could well have done without, as my services were rapidly drawing to a close. When I appeared with the wife, Lady Chamberlain said to her husband

'Who is this distinguished looking man coming towards us in the gorgeous uniform?'

Sir Neville looked and said, 'By Jove! he does look smart. I wonder who he is.'

As I came closer, however, he recognised me and said: –

'Why, hang it all, it's Waters, and he is wearing the same uniform as I have on myself.'

The mention of the medal I received in commemoration of this visit recalls an incident which occurred some years before, on the occasion of Queen Victoria's last visit to Ireland, when I also received a medal.[83] I was, at this time, in charge of the Crime Special department, and it was part of my duty to arrange for a staff of detectives for her protection. When she visited Dublin, I had men from all the principal towns in the South and West, who were well acquainted with the prominent suspects, and whose duty it was to keep a close eye on the movements of any of them who might be in the City. One man from a Southern town was believed to be specially dangerous; and he was shadowed wherever he went by two of my men. One morning, the Queen drove from the Viceregal Lodge, to the Castle, and a big crowd collected near the Park gates to see her go by. The suspect referred to was spotted in this crowd, shoving his way through the people, till he got right in front. My two men kept close, and took post behind him as the Queen came on. He stood quite silent and unmoved, until the Queen appeared; but, as she came close up, he suddenly took his hands out of his pockets, and one of the detectives had prepared to seize him, when he pulled off his hat, waved it wildly in the air, and shouted at the top of his voice: –

'Hurrah for the Queen. Long live Her Majesty, God bless her!'

So much for the influence Royalty had in Ireland when they chose to evoke it by a personal visit.

I come now to the end of my career in the RIC. Grateful I am that I saw it at its best, when its reputation still stood high, and it held a place in the esteem of all classes of people and of the Government which no other Police Force has ever excelled, and few indeed have equalled. Alas! the days of Its decadence were drawing near; and, even before I retired, the seed was being sown which soon grew into the crop of noxious weeds which eventually strangled it.

The authority of the uniformed officer of the law, which had been steadily maintained by British Governments for close on a hundred years, was slowly undermined by the weakness of the later executives; who taught the disaffected classes in Ireland the fatal lesson that the policeman was but an ordinary man after all, and that his truncheon had no more authority behind it, in critical times, than the blackthorn of any rowdy at a country fair. It must be recorded that this lesson was not altogether the work of liberal governments; nor was the poisonous seed sown in the South of Ireland alone. When the British Government winked at the arming of the Orangemen in the North, in revolt against a possible Act of the British Parliament, they opened the door to a similar arming of the disloyalists of the South, who were quite clever enough to see their opportunity and seize it, which they did, and thus undoubtedly lay the foundation of all the trouble which has befallen our country.

The action of Lord Aberdeen,[84] when Lord Lieutenant, in dismissing Mr. Harrel[85] from his post as Assistant Commissioner of Dublin Police, because he vigorously carried out his duty in the suppression of the importation of arms, thoroughly disheartened every Police Officer in Ireland.[86] No one knew if he would be supported in carrying out the requirements of law and order, as they have always been interpreted; and, as a consequence, the authority of the police steadily declined, as the audacity and activity of the Criminal conspirators gained strength.

I retired from the force on pension on the 23rd of October, 1906 having then served over 40 years. It was a remarkable stroke of luck for me that I had been appointed Sub-Inspector on the 10th June, 1866, and thus came under the conditions of service of an old Act of Parliament, which was superseded by an Act passed on the 1st July 1866. Under this later Act, I should only have been entitled to the Civil Service scale of pensions; whereas, under the old Act, I was entitled to retire on full pay. I was, I believe, the last official in Ireland to enjoy this privilege.[87]

At this time we were living in Adelaide Road, Dublin; and, as the family had scattered out and left the wife and I practically alone, we decided to give up the house, and seek a smaller abode elsewhere.

[*Waters's daughter and son-in-law provided them with the use of their summer cottage in Skerries.* Circa 60 words]

I had some debts, which I was anxious to wipe out; and to aid me in this, I jumped at an offer made to me by Mr. Walter Long,[88] on behalf of the Union Defence League.[89] This body was at a loss for rapid information to enable them to combat statements made in Parliament or in the Separatist press; and also for material for literature in support of the Union. I was asked to undertake to collect and furnish this information; and I was offered a salary which was extremely useful to me at the time. We settled down in the Skerries cottage, and here I took in a number of newspapers from all parts of the country. I culled from these journals reports of occurences, speeches &c., likely to attract notice, and, by my long association with the officers of the RIC, and the officials at the Castle, I was able to get facts and prepare for the Defence League memoranda, much as I had done for Mr. Arthur Balfour in other days. I wrote weekly articles for the 'Outlook',[90] which were afterwards published and circulated in pamphlet form.

We spent two very happy years in Skerries, and then my work for the Defence League came to an end, and we decided to look out for a house near Dublin. While in Skerries, I joined the Golf Club, and had many very pleasant rounds there, which, with my literary work, and a little shore shooting, passed the winter months very satisfactorily. We found the Skerries people very friendly, and the tradespeople very civil and obliging, though some of them had very primitive ideas of keeping accounts. For example, the lady who supplied us with fowl and vegetables was a Miss Mary Ann McLoughlin, who had very vague ideas as to book-keeping. She kept her accounts in hieroglyphics, intelligible to herself alone. On one occasion she billed the wife for two chickens which we never had. On being remonstrated with, she said: –

'Well, someone had them, and, as you are the best paying customer, I put them down to you.'

While looking round for a suitable abode, the wife and I took up our quarters at the Kilworth Hotel in Dublin, where we spent several months.

Eventually we decided to purchase the lease of Woodview, where I hope and trust we may be permitted to end our days in peace and quietness. When we first settled down, there was every prospect of this peaceful time. While in Skerries, I had cleared off all our debts; and we had enough in hand to do up the house, and complete its furniture. Until the black shadow of the Great War came over us, all was indeed well. Like every other loyal family in the country, the outbreak of hostilities called all of us to action one way or other. My two sons, Arthur and Dick, went to the front; Arthur in the Army Service Corps, and Dick as a driver of a Red Cross Ambulance. My eldest son, Bertie, was kept at Elswick, superintending the output of war material. Everyone had his job of some sort. Through the influence of John Noble, I was taken on in the Ministry of Munitions in London; and there I worked for several months, until things got so unsettled in Ireland that I felt I must go back and join the wife. During my stay in London, there were several bad air raids, and everyone was kept in constant alarm by these attacks. When leaving the Ministry of Munitions in London, I was led to believe I would be taken on in the Dublin office of the Ministry, then established in Nassau Street. I had introductions and strong recommendations to the heads of the Departments in Dublin. I found, however, I was not wanted there; and I had reason to know that my record as an officer of the RIC was against me. I hated to remain altogether idle; and, as I had my trusty old Ford car, I volunteered to drive for the Automobile Club in any war work which they required. I was told off for these classes of motor work: – to drive the Inspectors of Munitions to the different shell factories, stores and contractors' premises; to attend all hospital ships arriving at the North Wall, and convey wounded soldiers to the various hospitals, and also to drive convalescent soldiers from the hospitals twice a week to Balls Bridge, where the Automobile Club entertained them most hospitably. I attended at the North Wall on the arrival of every hospital ship which came in until the War ended, generally at early hours of the morning, in cold wintry weather, and I am glad to say I never was a pin the worse for the exposure.

Walter Johnstone had his work cut out as Chief Commissioner of the Dublin Police. The city was seething with sedition, which eventually culminated in the Rebellion of 1916. The seed sown by weakling Executives in Ireland had indeed done its work; and now the harvest of death and destruction was the result. The police, disheartened and discouraged by persistent neglect and contempt of their warnings, had lost their hold of information, and so the Easter week of 1916 came upon a Government uninformed, and unprepared to meet the outbreak.

The history of this rebellion has been told, and will be told, many times over. It forms no part of this Memoir. I had, fortunately nothing to do with it; though, when it was all over, I had some share in dealing with one of its results. When the British troops broke into Liberty Hall, they seized a great mass of books and documents, which were conveyed to the Castle, and placed in a cellar there. Ivon Price,[91] a County Inspector of RIC, was at this time attached to the Military Headquarters as an Intelligence Officer. He was asked to get someone to go through these records, classify them, and see if they contained any information of value. He asked me to undertake this job, which I did; and I got up two other RIC pensioned officers to help me.

We were given a room in the Chief Secretary's office, into which all the books and documents were carried. We spent some weeks there, carefully examining the documents, many of which were torn and many stained with blood. The military authorities hoped that we should find evidence, to be produced at the Court Martials, to be held on the rebels who had been captured, and were then in prison. Most of the papers consisted of correspondence with country branches of the extreme faction, and our labours had but little useful result.

When things had, to some extent settled down, I was asked by Sir John Taylor,[92] then Assistant Under-Secretary, to again start a sort of Intelligence Department at the Castle, to keep the Chief Secretary and the Irish Office in London in touch with what was happening in Ireland. I consented to give up my summer amusements, and once more

I began my job of cutting out press paragraphs and annotating them. At this time the scattered remnant of the Republican Army had devoted itself to establishing a reign of Terror, by the old methods of outrage on person and property. Cold blooded murders were frequent. The Viceroy of the day, Lord French,[93] was ambushed by an armed party, and barely escaped assassination.[94]

This led to one of the worst crimes of the period. The Government decided to start a secret inquiry under the Crimes Act, in the hope of getting evidence to convict the guilty parties. A very old friend of mine, Alan Bell,[95] a Resident Magistrate, was brought to Dublin to conduct the inquiry. He sat in a room next to me in the Castle; and we saw each other more or less every day. The circumstances of the murder are well known. He was, in open daylight, dragged out of a tram car at Balls Bridge, and shot dead, in the presence of a number of people, not one of whom raised a hand to help him. No one has ever been brought to justice for this murder. No effort was made to carry out the inquiry; and, indeed, it may be said that this murder of Alan Bell's put an end to any further attempt to deal with Irish Political crimes by the processes of ordinary law.[96] The life of every official of British Government was in danger; and, in a short time, many of them departed to safer regions. My work came to an end very soon after Alan Bell's death, and I have never since had anything to do with the Government of Ireland. The days of the effort of Britain to practically reconquer the south of the country by force of arms then began. The RIC proper, as a country Police force, was almost wiped out. Their isolated barracks were attacked in every direction; and although, in almost every case the rebels met with a stubborn resistance, the small parties of police had no chance against overwhelming numbers, organised and led by ex-soldiers, who had gained experience at the War in France and Belgium. Strong bodies of Military were imported and the police were reinforced by rapidly organised auxilliaries, who soon became known by the soubriquet of 'Black and Tans' from the colour of their uniform. I had personally nothing whatever to do with these auxiliaries; but it is certain that, while in isolated cases there were excesses committed, under great provocation here and there, the Black and Tans, on the whole, did good and loyal work; and many people in Ireland believe, and perhaps with justice, that if the British Government had not entered into a Treaty with the Southern rebels when it did, the military with the auxiliaries, would have settled the country.

All this is outside my personal history. I held on at Woodview with the wife through all the disturbances. Once the house was raided for arms by a masked and armed party. On several occasions similar parties came by night and day and carried off my good old Ford car which, however, was always returned more or less in a damaged condition. In this I was more fortunate than some of my neighbours, whose cars were taken and never returned. I made a virtue of necessity by yielding, with as good a grace as I could summon up, to these raiders, whom I was quite powerless to resist, and they in return, certainly brought me back the old bus, and only left me to pay for the repairs!

Of my personal history there is little now left to record. One by one our children have, in the natural course of events, dropped away from us; and the wife and I, in this good year of 1924, sit all alone at Woodview, — Darby — and Joan —, and very happy and very satisfied that we hold the love and affection of all our children, wherever they may be.

[*In order to maintain a spirit of family responsibility, Waters instituted a 'Family Order' in 1891 whereby he, his wife and his children entered into a lifetime 'bond of union' and vowed to assist other family members whenever needed and to look after each other's interests. He then recounts his associations with croquet and Freemasonry.* Circa 1,000 words]

There is little more to be said. The Memoirs come to an end. I am now in my seventy eighth year; and in the course of nature have little more to look forward to. Let me wind up with a hearty meed of thankfulness to the Providence which has carried me through so well.

I leave these papers to those who come after me to deal with as they may think fit.

Postscript written in August 1926

My poor wife passed away on the 7th June, 1926, leaving me lonely indeed.

Abbreviations

BL	British Library, London
CO	Colonial Office
CSO, RP	Chief Secretary's Office, Registered Papers
DMP	Dublin Metropolitan Police
HCP	House of Commons Papers
HO	Home Office
IC	Irish Constabulary
NAI	National Archives, Dublin
NLI	National Library of Ireland, Dublin
PRO	Public Record Office, London
RIC	Royal Irish Constabulary
(S)RM	(Special) Resident Magistrate
TCD	Trinity College, Dublin

Notes to Introduction

1 Before the establishment of the Peace Preservation Force, rural areas were policed by small forces of 'baronial constables' who were appointed and paid by county grand juries under parliamentary acts of 1787 and 1793.

2 Between 1836 and 1922 the strength of the Constabulary varied between 7,500 and 14,500, but its nominal strength was 10,000. Dublin had its own civil police force, the DMP, which was also established in 1836; by the time Waters joined the Constabulary in 1866 the DMP was the only other police force in Ireland. The Irish Constabulary was granted the prefix 'Royal' in 1867 for its role in suppressing the Fenian rising.

3 RIC Officers' Register: PRO, HO 184/45. In 1839 Chief Constables were renamed Sub-Inspectors, and in 1883 the rank was redesignated as District Inspector.

4 Rev. Mr Boyd to Inspector-General, 4 Nov. 1840; Viscount Morpeth to William Crozier, 7 Nov. 1840: NAI, CSO, RP 1840/I 14558; William Waters to Norman Macdonald, and Macdonald to Matthews, 18 Dec. 1840: ibid., CSO, RP 1840/I 16570.

5 RIC Officers' Register: PRO, HO 184/45.

6 Patrick Shea, *Voices and the Sound of Drums: An Irish Autobiography* (Belfast, 1981), p. 28.

7   In 1880 the RIC was composed of 3,209 Protestants (28 per cent) and 8,187 Roman Catholics (72 per cent). Of the 241 officers in the force, 193 were Protestants (80 per cent) and 48 were Catholics (20 per cent): HCP, 1880 (256), lix, 505–6.

8   Letters from 'Ex-RIC' and 'Ground Arms', *Irish Independent*, 10, 11 Feb. 1914. Catholic policemen also complained about the prevalence of Freemasonry among Protestant members of the force. Like many of his fellow officers, Samuel Waters was a Freemason. He joined the order in Enniskillen in the 1870s and subsequently passed the chair in the blue (craft) and red divisions. Freemasonry was the only oath-bound organisation to which Irish policemen were allowed to belong.

9   After 1867 one-fifth of officers were promoted from the ranks. In 1895 this quota was increased to one in two.

10 Four candidates were nominated for each vacancy as it occurred. The Inspector-General nominated one candidate in every three, usually a policeman's son, and the Chief Secretary or Lord Lieutenant nominated the other two. For further information on the selection of cadets see Jim Herlihy, *The Royal Irish Constabulary: A Short History and Genealogical Guide* (Dublin, 1997), pp. 83–4.

11 Brian Griffin, 'The Irish Police: A Social History, 1836–1914' (Ph.D. thesis, Loyola University, Chicago, 1990), p. 253.

12 For an account of cadet training in the nineteenth century see George Garrow Green, *In the Royal Irish Constabulary* (London, 1905), pp. 22–3.

13 J. W. Butler, RM, to Chief Secretary, 15 Apr. 1882: NAI, CSO, RP 1882/24328.

14 Page references in parentheses throughout the Introduction refer to the text of the following edition of Waters's memoirs.

15 David Harrel, 'Recollections and Reflections' (unpublished typescript, 1926): TCD, MS 3918a, ff. 3–4.

16 Monthly confidential report by Robert B. Stokes, Divisional Commissioner for the South-Western Division, June 1890: NAI, Crime Branch Special, 12093/S.

17 W. B. Yeats, 'In Memory of Eva Gore-Booth and Con Markiewicz' in *Collected Poems* (London, 1965 ed.), p. 263.

18 The children were named Edith, Lucy, Ethel, Maud, Helen, Amy, Florence, Violet, Cecile, Robert, Arthur, Richard and Olive.

19 Inspector-General John Stewart Wood to Under-Secretary, 1 Oct. 1870: NAI, CSO, RP 1870/18420.

20 RIC Officers' Register: PRO, HO 184/45. This offence was not uncommon. In 1869 the Inspector-General warned his officers against paying their men by cheque or promissory note, insisting that they be paid in cash. These incidents may account for Waters's peripatetic lifestyle. Recent research reveals that offending officers served in significantly more counties than officers with unblemished records. Waters's father seems to have been little better at fiscal management. When he

was County Inspector of Sligo in 1874, he was admonished for borrowing money from his subordinates. See Inspector-General's circular, 1 Jan. 1869: PRO, HO 184/114; Stanley Palmer, *Police and Protest in England and Ireland, 1780–1850* (Cambridge, 1988), p. 578.

21 As one recent historian of the RIC observes, 'most policemen spent most of their careers performing mundane, non-political tasks': Griffin, 'Irish Police', p. 810.

22 George A. Birmingham, 'Irishmen All, VII — The Policeman' in *The Outlook*, no. 18, xxxii (30 Aug. 1913), p. 287.

23 Ibid.

24 Ex-Head Constable Robert Mack to Lord Lieutenant, 18 May 1883: NAI, CSO, RP 1883/45668.

25 Alfred Webb, speech to the House of Commons, *Hansard 3*, cccxlvi, 1149–50 (8 July 1890).

26 William D'Arcy, *The Fenian Movement in the United States, 1858–1886* (Washington, DC, 1947); 'History of Fenianism': NLI, Larcom Papers, MS 7517. The leader of the expedition, John Warren, and his lieutenant, Augustine Costelloe, were tried before the Special Commission in October 1867 and sentenced to fifteen and twelve years' imprisonment respectively. The other prisoners admitted their guilt, expressed regret, and were allowed to return to America between August 1867 and May 1868. See 'Jackmel Prisoners', 19 May 1868: NLI, Mayo Papers, MS 11188 (15).

27 Burke was sentenced to fifteen years' imprisonment. He feigned insanity and was eventually released from Broadmoor Convict Lunatic Asylum in 1872. He returned to the United States to work as an engineer and became a member of Clan na Gael. See D. J. Hickey and J. E. Doherty, *A Dictionary of Irish History since 1800* (Dublin, 1980), p. 49.

28 J. W. Butler, RM, to Chief Secretary, 15 Apr. 1882: NAI, CSO, RP 1882/24328.

29 Waters was the first officer to use the Prevention of Crime Act of 1882. On 13 July 1882, the day after the act became law, Waters had Edward Connor summarily tried, convicted and sentenced to four months' hard labour for posting notices to deter bidding at the auction of a meadow on the property of Charles Battersby of Culvin, Co. Westmeath. See NAI, CSO, RP 1882/801 in RP 1882/4743; CSO, RP 1882/34539.

30 A. S. Butler, SRM, to Under-Secretary, 1 Jan. 1882: NAI, CSO, RP 1882/71 in RP 1882/1239; Butler to Burke, 15 Apr. 1882: ibid., CSO, RP 1882/18185 in RP 1882/19328; Sub-Inspector Samuel Waters to Inspector-General, 27 Feb. 1882: ibid., CSO, RP 1882/9866 in RP 1882/24578.

31 The case later became a *cause célèbre* when Cole retracted his evidence. The case was brought up several times in parliament, but the viceroy, Earl Spencer, refused to review the sentences. The Dublin journalist F. M. Bussy later claimed

that Curley, Fagan and Caffrey were hanged for their part in the Phoenix Park murders because the prosecuting authorities knew of their involvement in the Westmeath conspiracy. Confidential government records tend to support Bussy's claim. When Charles Stewart Parnell brought the Barbavilla case up in parliament in July 1885, a secret report was compiled which stated: 'Curley, before his execution for the Park murders, gave a full account to Mr Mallon, the detective superintendent, of his having attended the meeting at the Widow Fagan's, as afterwards sworn to by the McKeons.' See Frederick Moir Bussy, *Irish Conspiracies: Recollections of John Mallon, the Great Irish Detective, and Other Reminiscences* (London, 1910), pp. 132–3; 'Confidential Report on Cases referred to in Parnell's Motion', c. July 1885: BL, Althorp Papers, K. 495.

32   Hitherto the RIC had no full-time detectives outside Belfast, while the DMP had its own detective force. In October 1883, when the divisional system was reorganised, the Crime Department was divided into 'Ordinary' and 'Special' branches. The Crime Ordinary Branch handled 'all reports relating to outrages, the ordinary investigation of crime, the preservation of the peace, illegal assemblies and personal protection', while the Crime Special Branch collected and transmitted 'all secret information' and in very special cases assisted the local Constabulary in inquiries into cases of serious outrage. See E. G. Jenkinson to Divisional Magistrates, 1 Oct. 1883: NAI, CSO, RP 1883/22072.

33   The North-Western Division was created in March 1882. It consisted of Counties Mayo, Roscommon and Sligo. On 1 Oct. 1883 it was absorbed by the Midland and Western Divisions. See Inspector-General's circulars, 11 Mar. 1882, 1 Oct. 1883: PRO, HO 184/116.

34   Earl Spencer to William Harcourt, 27 Dec. 1883: BL, Althorp Papers, K. 17.

35   Although not a legal requirement, it was the custom in Ireland for judges to caution the jury that they should seek independent corroboration of any evidence given by an accomplice to a crime. The prosecution maintained that because Coleman had not been implicated in the conspiracy, he should have been treated as an independent witness. After the verdict was announced a 'scandalous scene' occurred, as the Attorney General, John Naish, openly remonstrated with the judge, William Johnson, his predecessor as Attorney General, over his conduct of the trial. See Harcourt to Spencer, 23 Dec. 1883: BL, Althorp Papers, K. 16; Spencer to Granville, 3 Feb. 1884: ibid., K. 17.

36   The newspapers in question were the *Roscommon Herald*, *Tuam News*, *Connaught Telegraph*, *Western People*, *Sligo Champion*, *Dundalk Democrat*, *People's Advocate*, *Kerry Sentinel*, *The Nationalist*, *Leinster Leader*, *Tipperary Advocate* and the *Wexford People*. See Waters to Inspector-General, 11 Mar. 1887: NAI, CSO, RP 1892/16059.

37   Many of these files were subsequently printed as the 'Intelligence Notes' which now provide a valuable source of information on the political history of Ireland

in the late nineteenth and early twentieth centuries. See 'Confidential Print, 1885–1919': PRO, CO 903/1–19.

38   On 7 March 1887, the day that Arthur Balfour became Irish Chief Secretary, *The Times* began to publish a series of articles which accused Parnell and other members of the Irish Parliamentary Party of direct involvement in agrarian crimes committed during the Land War of 1879–82. On 18 April the newspaper published a letter purporting to demonstrate Parnell's complicity in the Phoenix Park murders. In July 1887 F. H. O'Donnell, a former Home Rule MP, unsuccessfully sued *The Times* for libel. Parnell subsequently requested that a parliamentary select committee investigate the matter, but instead the government established a special parliamentary commission to conduct a judicial inquiry into the accusations. The commission sat between 17 September 1888 and 22 November 1889. The case against Parnell collapsed in February 1889 when the letter connecting Parnell to the Phoenix Park murders was shown to have been forged by Richard Pigott, on whose information the *Times* articles had been founded.

39   William Joyce later supplied documentary evidence of his role in the affair to Roger Casement. Waters was not alone in disbelieving the accusations against Parnell. The three men who led the police investigation into the Phoenix Park murders, David Harrel (Chief Commissioner of the DMP), John Mallon and Edward Jenkinson, all shared Waters's opinion, but none of them were called upon to give evidence before the commission. See Harrel, 'Recollections and Reflections', ff. 103–10; Leon Ó Broin, *The Prime Informer: A Suppressed Scandal* (London, 1971). For a recent analysis of the Special Commission see Margaret O'Callaghan, *British High Politics and a Nationalist Ireland: Criminality, Land and the Law Under Forster and Balfour* (Cork, 1994), pp. 112–20.

40   Nevertheless, there was considerable resentment among some police officers at the social elevation of leading nationalists. A Special Branch officer remarked that Edward Harrington 'is a typical successful agitator. He came to Kerry penniless. He now seems to have plenty of money and at times he spends it freely among his confreres in champagne': 'History of Suspects on the B List': NAI, Crime Branch Special, 1181/S.

41   The idea that the Irish secret service was run down after 1900 has been dismissed by one recent historian as a 'unionist shibboleth'. However, Sir Antony Mac-Donnell, the Under-Secretary between 1902 and 1908, was extremely sceptical of the value of the Special Branch and did scale down police operations. In July 1920 Sir Nevil Macready, the Commander-in-Chief in Ireland, told the Chief Secretary that the only sources of police information in Ireland 'since the Secret Service was practically abolished in 1906' had been the 'corner boys and loafers' who had recently defected to Sinn Féin. See Eunan O'Halpin, 'British Intelligence in Ireland, 1914–1921' in Christopher Andrew and David Dilks (eds), *The Missing*

Dimension: Governments and Intelligence Communities in the Twentieth Century (London, 1984), pp. 54–77; Eunan O'Halpin, *The Decline of the Union: British Government in Ireland 1892–1920* (Dublin, 1987), pp. 62–4; Sir Nevil Macready to Chief Secretary, 17 July 1920: PRO, CO 904/188, f. 427.

Notes to Narrative

1 George Walker (c.1646–1690), Church of Ireland clergyman. Walker did not 'close the gates' of Derry, though he acted as joint city governor during the siege by the Jacobite supporters of King James II, April–July 1689. Walker was killed at the battle of the Boyne in 1690.

2 Sir Robert Peel (1788–1850), 2nd Bart, Chief Secretary for Ireland, 1812–18; Home Secretary, 1822–27, 1828–30; Prime Minister, 1834–35, 1841–46.

3 Sir Duncan McGregor (b. 1787), Inspector-General, IC, 1838–58.

4 Nathan & Son of Houndsditch.

5 Thomas Montgomery (1842–73), Sub-Inspector, RIC, 1866–72. Montgomery, the son of a police officer, had been an accountant for eight years in the Belfast Bank before joining the Constabulary. In March 1871 he was posted to Newtownstewart, Co. Tyrone. On 29 June William Glass, a cashier in the local branch of the Northern Bank, was found murdered in the bank office. He had been struck in the head repeatedly with a hedge slasher, and £1,600 had been taken from the cash box. At the inquest a verdict of wilful murder was found against Montgomery, and he was committed for trial at the 1872 spring assizes in Omagh. Montgomery was tried three times before finally being found guilty in July 1873, and he was hanged in Omagh jail in November 1873. See 'Return of Outrages reported to the Constabulary Office in Ireland during the year 1871, with Summaries for Preceding Years': NAI, CSO, RP 1872/1864 in RP 1873/205). For an account of Montgomery's trial see 'An Unparalleled Murder' in Matthias McDonnell Bodkin, *Famous Irish Trials* (Dublin, 1918; new ed. Dublin, 1997), pp. 95–103.

6 Sir Robert Gore-Booth (1805–76), 4th Bart, MP for Co. Sligo, 1850–76.

7 Thomas Lindley (b. 1818), Head Constable, IC and RIC. A former labourer from Armagh, Lindley joined the Constabulary in 1838. He was promoted to Head Constable in 1861 and posted to Grange, where he remained until his retirement in 1875. See RIC General Register: PRO, HO 184/2.

8 Colonel George Hillier, Inspector-General, RIC, 1876–82.

9 Colonel Sir John Stewart Wood, Inspector-General, IC and RIC, 1865–76.

10 The Inspector-General issued three memoranda between March 1868 and April 1869 expressing his disappointment with the force's failure to detect serious

offences such as murder, burglary, arson and cattle stealing. He prevailed upon all Sub-Inspectors to improve the detective qualities of the force by regularly examining their men on the steps to be taken for detecting criminals. See 'Memorandum', 14 Mar. 1868; 'Memoranda II', 26 Mar. 1868; 'Memorandum III', 12 Apr. 1869: PRO, HO 184/114.

11 Charles Bradstreet Wynne (1835–90), Major, 90th Light Infantry and Sligo Rifles, Clerk of the Peace for Sligo. Married Emily Frances Graham, eldest daughter of Sir Robert Gore-Booth.

12 On 8 September 1855, during the seige of Sebastapol, the 2nd Brigade of the Light Division stormed the Great Redan, the largest of the fortified earthworks defending the town. Having taken the position, they were forced to evacuate it under heavy fire at the cost of nearly 2,500 casualties. In May 1857, during the Indian Mutiny, a small British force set out to recapture Delhi. The column became itself besieged outside the city before being relieved some weeks later.

13 Colonel Ricard Burke (1838–1922), Irish-American Fenian.

14 After a protracted inquest into the death of Captain King, the coroner's jury returned an open verdict. It was believed that the fatal shot had been fired accidentally by his colleague Mr Webster. See *Sligo Chronicle*, 5 Dec. 1868; NAI, CSO, RP 1868/18276.

15 Daniel Jennings, County Inspector, RIC, Clare, 1866–72, Dublin, 1872–82.

16 The act referred to was officially entitled the Peace Preservation (Ireland) Act, 1870.

17 The Lady Day confrontation at Kilrea was an annual occurrence which usually required the presence of between 50 and 100 policemen. In 1874 400 Constabulary and 40 cavalrymen were needed to keep the peace: HCP, 1880 (380), lx, 395.

18 Constabulary Sub-Inspectors were given an allowance of 9d per mile when travelling outside their districts to attend assizes.

19 Samuel Plimsoll (1824–98), Radical MP for Derby, 1868–80. Known as 'the Sailors' Friend', he was responsible for expediting the passage of the Merchant Shipping Act, 1876.

20 The *Cardross* was a 568-ton sailing ship which capsized off Cape Clear on the night of 10 February 1874 with the loss of sixteen lives. During its return journey to Liverpool with a cargo of mahogany from Nicaragua the ship took on water and had to put in at Queenstown. After the ship capsized the crew clung to the rigging for thirty-four hours before the ship broke up. Only two crew members survived. The inquiry into the wreck was held at Greenwich police court between 27 March and 29 April 1874. See *The Times*, 12 Mar., 30 Apr. 1874.

21 According to the Merchant Shipping Act, 1854, when a wreck was salvaged by the Constabulary the owners were liable to pay them a reasonable amount of

salvage. See *Standing Rules and Regulations for the Government and Guidance of the Royal Irish Constabulary* (3rd ed., Dublin, 1872), app. 24, pp. 384–6.

22 Timothy Charles Harrington (1851–1910), Secretary of the Irish National League, MP for Westmeath, 1883–85, and Dublin Harbour, 1885–1910, Lord Mayor of Dublin, 1901–4.

23 Henry George Carey (b. 1836), County Inspector, RIC, Fermanagh, 1876–82, and Armagh, 1884–87.

24 William Edward Forster (1818–86), Chief Secretary for Ireland, 1880–82.

25 Protection of Person and Property (Ireland) Act, 1881.

26 Henry Jephson, Private Secretary to the Chief Secretary for Ireland, 1880–82.

27 Michael Davitt (1846–1906), Fenian, founder of the Land League, MP for North Meath, 1892, North-East Cork, 1893, and South Mayo, 1895–99.

28 Harrington was sentenced on 11 January 1883 to two months' imprisonment for a speech he made on behalf of farm labourers on 17 December 1882 at a National League meeting in Mullingar. He was elected MP for Westmeath on 24 February 1883.

29 Sir Edward George Jenkinson (1835–1919), Indian Civil Service, 1856–80; Assistant Under-Secretary for Police and Crime, 1882–86.

30 When Jenkinson succeeded Sir Henry Brackenbury as head of the Irish police organisation in August 1882, there were six police divisions in Ireland, each of them under the charge of a 'Special Resident Magistrate'. These officers were redesignated 'Divisional Magistrates' in October 1883, but they were not given the title of 'Divisional Commissioner' until 1889. The post was abolished in 1898 and revived for a short time in 1920.

31 Arthur Swords, Bernard Ryan, Bryan Fitzpatrick, Robert Elliot and Michael McGrath were tried at the Dublin commission in April 1884; charged with conspiracy to murder, they were each sentenced to ten years' imprisonment. William McCormack, John Fagan, Pat Fagan, John Boyhan and James Gaffney were tried in June 1884, and each was imprisoned for seven years. An eleventh defendant, John McGrath, was sent to prison for one year. See 'Return of Outrages reported to the Constabulary Office in Ireland during the year 1884, with Summaries for Preceding Years': NAI, CSO, RP 1886/1861.

32 John W. E. Dunsterville (b. 1851), District Inspector, RIC, 1870–85, Resident Magistrate, 1885–1916.

33 Colonel Robert Bruce (1825–99), Inspector-General, RIC, 1882–85.

34 Colonel William Forbes, Special Resident Magistrate, North-Western Division, 1882–83.

35 Thomas Hayes (b. 1845), District Inspector, RIC, 1866–98, County Inspector, 1898–1905.

36   Fredrick James Ball (b. 1851), District Inspector, RIC, 1877–99, County Inspector, 1899–1908, Assistant Inspector-General, 1908–12. The informer's name was Andrew Coleman.

37   After the jury failed to reach a verdict at Cork winter assizes in November 1883, the seven men were re-tried for conspiracy to murder at the spring assizes in Cork in March 1884. T. A. McCawley, P. W. Nally and Thomas Daly were each sentenced to ten years' imprisonment; Peter Monnelly received seven years, and James King and Matthew Melvin were each imprisoned for five years. See 'Return of Outrages reported to the Constabulary Office in Ireland during the year 1884, with Summaries for Preceding Years': NAI, CSO, RP 1886/1861.

38   Sir Andrew Reed (1837–1914), Divisional Magistrate, Western Division, 1883–85, Inspector-General, RIC, 1885–1900.

39   John Donville Phillips (1847–84), District Inspector, RIC, 1872–84.

40   The Sherwood Foresters' hospitality soon became notorious. On 6 May 1884 Thomas Sexton, MP, accused Captain Beckett, the Resident Magistrate in Athlone, of conducting his business from the military mess and going on a drunken rampage with the regiment's officers. The charges were denied. See Beckett to Hamilton, 4 May 1884: NAI, CSO, RP 1884/10625; *Hansard 3*, cclxxxvii, 1478–9 (6 May 1884).

41   In order to avoid any friction, Waters not given charge of Special Branch work in Belfast. Crime detection there remained under the supervision of the Town Inspector, Mr Townshend. See E. G. Jenkinson to Lord Lieutenant, 10 Mar. 1885: BL, Althorp Papers, K. 39.

42   Sir William Squire Barker Kaye (1831–1901), Assistant Under-Secretary for Ireland, 1878–95.

43   The Special Branch had at its disposal 'special' men, usually sergeants or Head Constables, who were engaged full-time on detective work, and 'selected' constables who were employed temporarily as detectives when required.

44   Sir Redvers Henry Buller (1839–1908), Special Commissioner for Kerry and Clare, 1886; Under-Secretary for Ireland, 1886–87; Commander-in-Chief, South African War, 1899.

45   Sir Robert George Crookshank Hamilton (1836–95), Under-Secretary for Ireland, 1882–86; Governor of Tasmania, 1886–93.

46   Waters met Buller at the Railway Hotel in Killarney on 5 September 1886 and briefed the new Commissioner on the organisation of the Special Branch. See Buller to Hicks Beach, 5 Sept. 1886: Gloucester Record Office, St Aldwyn Papers, D2455, PCC/45.

47   Sir Alfred Turner (1842–1918), Special Commissioner for Kerry and Clare, 1886–92.

48 Evictions had taken place at Glenbeigh in November 1885, and Waters undertook his peace-making mission with Turner during the second week of September 1886. However, more evictions took place at Glenbeigh between 11 and 28 January 1887. The land agent's insistence on burning down the evicted cabins led to a riot, during which twenty-five people were arrested. The evictions were bitterly criticised by the National League, and protest meetings were held in Cork and Killorglin. See *The Times*, 13, 15, 19, 22, 24, 26, 31 Jan. 1887.

49 On 13 December 1885 Jeremiah Rahilly was beaten to death a short distance outside Killarney. He was a caretaker on an evicted farm at Knockasartnert. See *The Times*, 15 Dec. 1885.

50 Arthur James Balfour (1848–1930), 1st Earl of Balfour, Chief Secretary for Ireland, 1887–91; Prime Minister, 1902–5.

51 George Wyndham (1863–1913), Private Secretary to Chief Secretary for Ireland, 1887–91; Chief Secretary for Ireland, 1900–5.

52 Between 29 March 1888 and 19 February 1891 George Wyndham wrote a series of letters to *The Times* in which he refuted allegations made by Liberal and Irish Nationalist politicians against the authorities in Ireland. See *Life and Letters of George Wyndham*, ed. J. W. Mackail and Guy Wyndham (2 vols, London, 1925), i, 41–3; see also *The Times*, 29 Mar, 20 Dec. 1888, 9 Jan., 10 Aug., 19 Nov. 1889, 17 Nov. 1890, 19 Feb. 1891.

53 Dodgson Hamilton Madden (1840–1928), Solicitor General, 1888–89; Attorney General, 1889–92; Judge of the Queen's Bench Division, 1892–1919.

54 Sir George Otto Trevelyan (1838–1928), 2nd Bart, Chief Secretary for Ireland, 1882–84.

55 On 8 November 1883, while Waters was away on duty in Athlone, the dispensary medical officer, Thomas Salmon, attended Mrs Waters in a negligent manner. Waters subsequently accused the doctor of drunkenness and malpractice. Following an inquiry, the Local Government Board requested Salmon's resignation: NAI, CSO, RP 1884/6815.

56 Charles Stewart Parnell (1846–91), President of the Irish National Land League, 1879–82, and the Irish National League, 1882–91; Chairman of the Irish Parliamentary Party, 1880–90.

57 Richard Pigott (1828–89), journalist, proprietor of *The Irishman*, 1865–81.

58 Alfred E. Horne, Sub-Inspector, IC and RIC, 1865–82; Resident Magistrate, 1882–1908.

59 Pigott fled to Madrid where he was confronted by British police and committed suicide on 29 February 1889.

60 James Samuel Gibbons (1850–1914), District Inspector, RIC, 1868–91, County Inspector, 1891–95.

61   Richard Edmund St Lawrence Boyle (1829–1904), 9th Earl of Cork and Orrery. He owned 38,500 acres which included an 11,500-acre estate in Co. Kerry.

62   William John Loftie (ed.), *Orient Line Guide: Chapters for Travellers by Sea and by Land . . . for the Voyage between England and Australia* (4th ed., London, 1890).

63   In fact Hamilton's Home Rule sympathies led the Conservative government to replace him with Buller in December 1886, three months before Balfour was appointed Chief Secretary.

64   Edward Harrington, MP for West Kerry, 1885–92.

65   Sir Walter Edgeworth-Johnstone (1863–1936), Lieutenant-Colonel, Royal Irish Regiment; RM, 1904–15, Chief Commissioner, DMP, 1915–23.

66   Lord Ventry's gamekeeper, Edward Boyle, had been boycotted since 1880. In November 1882 he survived an assassination attempt and remained under police protection for many years. Protection was re-established for Boyle in December 1894, when he gave evidence at the trial of John Twiss, who was subsequently hanged for the murder of James Donovan. The officer who first arranged Boyle's protection described him as 'a drunken sot'. See Heffernan Considine, RM, to T. O. Plunkett, SRM, 1 Dec. 1882: NAI, CSO, RP 1882/47083; Divisional Commissioner's monthly confidential report, South-Western Division, Jan. 1895: ibid., Crime Branch Special, Police and Crimes Records, Divisional Commissioner's and County Inspector's monthly confidential reports, carton 4.

67   John Morley (1838–1923), Viscount Morley of Blackburn, Chief Secretary for Ireland, 1886, 1892–95.

68   Sir Lawrence Charles Edward Downing Dowdall (1851–1936), assistant private secretary to Arthur Balfour, 1887–92, John Morley, 1892–95, Gerald Balfour, 1895–1900, and George Wyndham, 1900–1.

69   Sir Robert Baret Stokes (1833–99), Divisional Commissioner, RIC, South-Eastern Division, 1893–98.

70   Garnet Joseph Wolseley (1833–1913), Viscount Wolseley, Commander-in-Chief of the British army, 1895–99.

71   Colonel Neville Chamberlain (1856–1944), Inspector-General, RIC, 1900–16.

72   In fact Wyndham was appointed Chief Secretary after the Conservative government was returned to power in October 1900. Balfour succeeded Lord Salisbury as Prime Minister in July 1902.

73   The Wyndham Land Purchase Act, 1903, offered an incentive to landlords to sell their estates to their tenants by offering them a state-subsidised bonus. The act brought about a major change in the Irish landholding system.

74   Lord Edward FitzGerald (1763–98), son of the 1st Duke of Leinster, a leader of the United Irishmen. George Wyndham was his great-grandson.

75   Sir Antony MacDonnell (1844–1925), Baron MacDonnell, entered Indian civil service, 1865; Chief Commissioner of Central Provinces, 1890–95; Lieutenant-

Governor of North-Western Provinces and Oudh, 1895–1901; Under-Secretary for Ireland, 1902–8.

76   Heffernan Considine (1846–1912), Deputy Inspector-General, RIC, 1900–11.

77   Sir Henry Thynne (1838–1915), Deputy Inspector-General, RIC, 1886–1900.

78   In March 1905 MacDonnell told the Chief Secretary, Walter Long: 'During 2½ years of careful observation I have not seen a particle of substantial evidence to show that there is in Ireland any secret political activity of which the Government need have the smallest apprehension': MacDonnell to Chief Secretary, 20 Mar. 1905: NAI , Crime Branch Special, 29989/S.

79   Edward VII was in Ireland between 26 April and 4 May 1904. He visited Kilkenny on 30 April.

80   James Edward William Theobald Butler (1844–1919), 3rd Marquess of Ormond.

81   John Daly (1845–1916) led the raid on Kilmallock barracks during the Fenian rising in 1867; imprisoned for dynamite offences in 1884; Lord Mayor of Limerick, 1899–1901.

82   Patrick Hoyne.

83   A total of 7,700 bronze commemorative medals were issued to all officers and men of the RIC who were on duty in Dublin on the occasion of the visit of Edward VII between 21 July and 1 August, 1903, and 2,300 medals were issued on the occasion of Queen Victoria's last visit to Ireland between 3 April and 26 April 1900. See Herlihy, *Royal Irish Constabulary*, pp. 93–6.

84   John Campbell Hamilton Gordon (1847–1934), 1st Marquess of Aberdeen and Temair, Lord Lieutenant of Ireland, 1886, 1905–15.

85   William Vesey Harrel (1866–1956), Assistant Commissioner, DMP, 1902–14.

86   On 26 July 1914 Harrel sent a force of police and troops to prevent the distribution of arms landed at Howth by the Irish Volunteers. In the resulting affray in Bachelor's Walk, Dublin, soldiers shot dead four members of the crowd.

87   The act of 1847 (10 & 11 Vict., c. 100) allowed officers of forty years' service to retire on full pay. On 10 August 1866 this arrangement was changed by another act (29 & 30 Vict., c. 103) which restricted the pension to three-fifths of full pay, available after thirty years' service.

88   Walter Hume Long (1854–1924), 1st Viscount Long of Wraxall, Chief Secretary for Ireland, 1905; leader of the Irish Unionist Party, 1906–10.

89   The Union Defence League was founded by Walter Long in 1907 to organise anti-Home Rule propaganda in Great Britain.

90   The *Outlook* was a Conservative and Unionist weekly review established by George Wyndham in February 1898 to promote imperial trade policies.

91   Ivon H. Price (1866–1931), District Inspector, RIC, 1891–1914; seconded as Director of Military Intelligence, 1914–18; County Inspector, RIC, Cavan and Fermanagh, 1919–20; Assistant Inspector-General, RIC, 1920–22.

92 Sir John James Taylor (1859–1945), Assistant Under-Secretary for Ireland, 1918–20.

93 John Denton Pinkstone French (1852–1925), 1st Earl of Ypres, Field-Marshal, Lord Lieutenant of Ireland, 1918–21.

94 The ambush took place at Ashtown, Co. Dublin, on 19 December 1919.

95 Alan Bell (1857–1920), District Inspector, RIC, 1879–98, Resident Magistrate, 1898–1920.

96 Alan Bell was brought to Dublin Castle in November 1919 as a counter-intelligence officer for the Directorate of Intelligence at Scotland Yard. He investigated the Ashtown ambush and the assassination of Inspector Redmond, the DMP's senior investigator of political offences. Bell was tracing Sinn Féin and Dáil Éireann funds when he was shot dead by members of Michael Collins's 'Squad' on 26 March 1920. See O'Halpin, *Decline of the Union*, pp. 198–9; Tim Pat Coogan. *Michael Collins: A Biography* (London, 1990), p. 188.

Bibliography

Ball, Stephen, 'Policing the Land War: British Government Policy towards Political Protest and Agrarian Crime in Ireland, 1879–92' (Ph.D. thesis, Goldsmith's College, University of London, 1999)

Breathnach Séamus, *The Irish Police—From the Earliest Times to the Present Day* (Dublin, 1974)

Brewer, John D., *The Royal Irish Constabulary: An Oral History* (Belfast, 1990)

Bridgeman, Ian R., 'Policing Rural Ireland: A Study of the Origins, Development, and Role of the Irish Constabulary and its Impact on Crime Prevention and Detection in the Nineteenth Century (Ph.D. thesis, Open University, 1993)

Broeker, Galen, *Rural Disorder and Police Reform in Ireland, 1812–1836* (London, 1970)

Brophy, Michael, *Sketches of the Royal Irish Constabulary* (London, 1886)

Crossman, Virginia, *Politics, Law and Order in Nineteenth-Century Ireland* (Dublin, 1996)

Curtis, Robert, *The History of the Royal Irish Constabulary* (London, 1869)

Duggan, G. C., 'The Royal Irish Constabulary' in Owen Dudley Edwards and Fergus Pyle (eds), *1916: The Easter Rising* (London, 1968), pp. 91–9

Fedorowich, Kent, 'The Problems of Disbandment: The Royal Irish Constabulary and imperial migration, 1919–1929, *Irish Historical Studies*, xxx, no. 117 (May, 1996), pp. 88–110

Fitzpatrick, David, *Politics and Irish Life: Provincial Experience of War and Revolution, 1913–1921* (2nd ed., Cork, 1998)

Fulham, Gregory J., James Shaw Kennedy and the Reformation of the Irish Constabulary, 1836–1838, *Éire–Ireland*, xvi (1981), pp. 93–106

Gaughan, J. Anthony (ed.), *The Memoirs of Constable Jeremiah Mee, R.I.C.* (Dublin, 1975)

Green, George Garrow, *In the Royal Irish Constabulary* (London, 1905)

Griffin, Brian, 'The Irish Police, 1836–1914: A Social History' (Ph.D. thesis., Loyola University of Chicago, 1990)

—— 'Religion and Opportunity in the Irish Police Forces, 1836–1914' in R. V. Comerford *et al* (eds), *Religion, Conflict and Coexistence in Ireland: Essays [presented to Monsignor Patrick J. Corish* (Dublin, 1990), pp. 219–34

Hawkins, Richard, 'Dublin Castle and the Royal Irish Constabulary 1916–1922' in T. Desmond Williams (ed.), *The Irish Struggle* (London, 1966), pp. 167–81

—— 'The Irish Model and the Empire: A Case for Reassessment' in David Anderson and David Killingray (eds), *Policing the Empire* (Manchester, 1991), pp. 18–32

Herlihy, Jim, *Royal Irish Constabulary: A Complete Alphabetical List of Officers and Men, 1816–1922* (Dublin, 1999)

—— *The Royal Irish Constabulary: A Short History and Genealogical Guide* (Dublin, 1997)

Lowe, W.J., Policing Famine Ireland, *Eire–Ireland*, xxix, (1994), pp. 47–67

—— 'The Constabulary Agitation of 1882', *Irish Historical Studies*, xxxii, no. 121 (May 1998), pp. 37–59

—— and Malcolm, Elizabeth, 'The Domestication of the Royal Irish Constabulary', *Irish Economic and Social History*, xix (1992), pp. 27–48

McEldowney, John F., Policing and the Administration of Justice in Nineteenth-Century Ireland' in Clive Emsley and Barbara Weinberger (eds.) *Policing Western Europe:Politics, Professionalism, and Public Order, 1850–1940* (Westport Conn., 1991), pp. 18–35

Ó Ceallaigh, Tadhg, Peel and Police Reform in Ireland, 1814–18', *Studia Hibernica*, vi (1966), pp. 25–48

Palmer, Stanley, *Police and Protest in England and Ireland, 1780–1850* (Cambridge, 1988)

Townshend, Charles, *Political Violence in Ireland: Government and Resistance since 1848* (Oxford, 1983)

Index

Printed in the United Kingdom
by Lightning Source UK Ltd.
106175UKS00001B/1-120